"THE WRITING OF THIS I
taken great pains to stay tru
even down to the beauty of
will enjoy the high language
artee ... Lovers of words wil
that exceeds the tweet, eleva ... charges the mind."

- Andrea Johnson, *Front Row Reviewers*

"A DELIGHTFUL PLAY."

- Harlow Clark, *A Motley Vision*

"I FELT AS THOUGH I WAS WATCHING A PLAY THE ENGLISH-SPEAKING WORLD HAD BEEN WAITING 400 YEARS FOR ... Stewart weaves a rich tapestry that even the Bard would delight in ... I felt like I was encountering a long-lost and newly rediscovered Shakespearean play ... the true magic of Stewart's play is that he successfully replicates Shakespeare's uncanny ability to peer into and convincingly play with timeless human nature."

- Hillary Stirling, AML/*Dawning of a Brighter Day*

Mahonri Stewart is an award-winning writer and educator. He has written over two dozen plays, most of which have been produced throughout the U.S. and Europe, including productions in Los Angeles, Scotland, and Switzerland. In 2004, his premiere play *Farewell to Eden* won the Kennedy Center's American College Theater Festival's National Playwriting Award (Second Place) and their National Selection Team Fellowship Award. Since then he has also received numerous other awards and honors for his plays, and strives to expand his writing into various other mediums. He received his MFA in Theatre: Dramatic Writing from Arizona State University and his Bachelor degree in Theatre Arts from Utah Valley Univeristy. He is a former Playwright-in-Residence at the Noorda Regional Theater.

The Drownèd Book

Or, The History of William Shakespeare

Part Last

A PLAY BY MAHONRI STEWART

Mahonri Stewart
The Drownéd Book: Or, The History of William Shakespeare, Part Last.

Published by: Prospero Arts and Media

Text Design by: Mahonri Stewart

Cover Art by: Trevor Downs

ISBN-13: 978-1723095207
ISBN-10: 1723095206

For performance rights to *The Drownéd Book*, **contact Prospero Arts and Media at prosperoarts@gmail.com.**

CHARACTERS

(In Order of Appearance)

WILLIAM SHAKESPEARE, near the end of his life
HAMNET'S GHOST, as he was when he died, 11 years old
THOMAS QUINEY
JUDITH SHAKESPEARE
ANNE SHAKESPEARE
SUSANNA SHAKESPEARE
JOHN HALL

From left to right: Sam Schofield as Thomas Quiney, Zel Bromley as Judith Shakespeare, Shawnda Moss as Anne Shakespeare, Bradley Moss as William Shakespeare, and Belinda Purdum as Susanna Shakespeare.
Photo by Emily Drew.

THE DROWNÈD BOOK

Or, The History of William Shakespeare, Part Last

A play by Mahonri Stewart

Originally presented in Provo, UT, at the Castle Amphitheater, on August 25, 2017, by Zion Theater Company. The Cast was as follows:

William Shakespeare	Bradley Moss
Anne Shakespeare	Shawnda Moss
Judith Shakespeare	Zel Bromley
Thomas Quiney	Sam Schofield
Susanna Shakespeare	Belinda Purdum
John Hall	Peter F. Christensen
Hamnet's Ghost	Hyrum Stewart

Director	Mahonri Stewart
Stage Managers	Ashley Kelly Katherine Gaylord

For Anne:
My Hermione, My Beatrice, My Juliet, My Imogen,
My Viola.

For Hyrum:
My Prince Hal, My Puck, My Questioning Hamlet.

For Charlotte:
My Marina, My Cordelia, My Miranda.

Bradley Moss as William Shakespeare (foreground).
Hyrum Stewart as Hamnet's Ghost (background).
Photo by Emily Drew.

"More are men's ends marked than their lives before:
The setting sun, and music at the close,
As the last taste of sweets, is sweetest last,
Writ in remembrance more than things long past."
- *Richard II*

"The web of our life is of a mingled yarn, good and ill together: our virtues would be proud, if our faults whipped them not; and our crimes would despair, if they were not cherished by our virtues."
- *All's Well That Ends Well*

"O my good lord, when I was like this maid,
I found you wondrous kind...
Will you be mine, now you are doubly won?"
- *All's Well That Ends Well*

"...But this rough magic
I here abjure, and, when I have required
Some heavenly music, which even now I do,
To work mine end upon their senses that
This airy charm is for, I'll break my staff,
Bury it certain fathoms in the earth,
And deeper than did ever plummet sound
I'll drown my book."
- *The Tempest*

The Drownèd Book
Or, The History of William Shakespeare, Part Last

~ I. 1 *Stratford Upon Avon, England. The action of the play is a conflation of the events that happen between the years 1607-1616. Enter WILLIAM SHAKESPEARE.*

WILLIAM

(Aside:)

There it is, paradise and purgatory,
My rest, my wrack, Stratford Upon Avon.
Longing and loathing, place of sharp mem'ry;
Such pointed mem'ry 'tis a potent mixture,
An alchemist's attempt to have both ways,
Gold and iron, comfort and weighty chain.

(Enter HAMNET, Shakespeare's ghostly son, age 11.)

Ah, you have come again, as I had thought,
To spur me on, my dear, airy lion,
Little sprite, small spirit, made of fast fire,
Have you once more come to refine desire?

HAMNET Joy.

WILLIAM

Such heft in such a tiny word, in joy.
How can I enjoin in joy, enjoy that joy,
When my sad heart feels heavy, so infirm?
Wilt thou bring me with thee to thy high place,
To see if my heart fares better up there?

HAMNET Joy.

WILLIAM

Is that thy message whole, all thou canst say?

HAMNET Joy.

WILLIAM

Joy to whom, Joy with whom, from whom, on whom?

I have sought joy in all the twisted paths,

For it doth still evade my entreaties!

(Exit Hamnet.)

Gone.

If I could but tear down Heaven's tall tree,

And bring thee back to those who love and live

That miss thee. Yet thou art more free up there.

I will remember thee, who could forget,

Seeing the one on whom his heart has set?

(Enter THOMAS QUINEY, bumping Shakespeare.)

Pardon me, sir, I did not see thee there!

QUINEY

And yet I saw thee, we all do see thee,

Master of Stratford, Prodigal repaired;

From my youth I have seen thee and despaired.

WILLIAM

Do I know thee, sir?

QUINEY Not a whit, sirrah.

You know not else, 'cept what Narcissus knew.

WILLIAM

I see thou art not civil

QUINEY Should I be?

Civility brings peace; I want a brawl.

WILLIAM

Why wouldst thy mind have aught of me at all?

I know thee not.

QUINEY And yet I know thy face.

If I could but mawl its monstrous features!

WILLIAM

If thou hadst caught me in my younger days,
I would do more than bite my thumb, dear sir,
I would bite thine; but I aim for peace now,
So shall cool my blood and say gramercy
For thy most gracious and good company.

Exit William.

QUINEY

(Aside:)

Thou didst see that burr of a cur, that scut?
That logger head who vainly claims wisdom?
That sly hedgepig whose quills he pretends smooth?
That onion nose, swag-bellied, dank Shag-speare?
Surely thou hast been told of his bright fame,
Hot-wrought fortune made of paper and ink,
Which alchemists formed into breathing golems.
If thou hast not heard of him, then go ask
That Moldwarp vain and he inform thee shall!
That rakehell hath not skills that he boasts of!
Whilst I was once in London with my sire,
I witnessed some of his wrought-over plays.
My old parent sung him as something great,
Ovid born again in English form,
And from our humble Stratford-born, to wit!
Yet when I watchéd those bland, mewling players
Perform those travesti of tragedies,
I could not help but make sport at his words!
I laughed at deaths, and wept at all the jests!

Thus, mortified was I when my old sire
Went to that weak, milk-livered, gleeking actor
And fawned, abased himself so that he could
Purloin some money from that frog, that toadstool.
Shame burned to see my patriarch thus kneeling
'Fore a player! It was he who shouldst kneel!
Break-speare feigned to feel for my poor forebear,
Granting the pitiful and shaméd request,
As if his pretense false was draped in alms,
Benevolance, in blesséd charity!
Such false agapé I forthwith abjure!
I knew his dye, that shade beneath his false love!
A sly Wolf-Sheep, a con, a pseudo-Jew!
Like his own Shylock, his copy, laid traps,
Trading curs´d coins for a pound of flesh.
Good fortune it was then my father died
Before such usuary could be complete
And later come so fully, bloody due.
Believe you Shakes the saint, great man of words?
If sincerity be found in that scratch
'Tis because he stole words, called them his.
Traffic I forswore with verbs of folly,
Thus, would I then nurse tobacco and ale,
Entertain the Jade upon happy knee,
Or be witness, of bear or bull thus baited,
Rather than see Will's plays over-rated.

(Enter JUDITH SHAKESPEARE.)

If that clay-brained canary hath not skill
With art and beauty bold, signed by cold Bill,
There is yet one form his flesh can fine-craft:
He wrought a bonnie girl, that keen Shake-shaft.

(To Judith:)

Good morrow, Mistress Shakespeare, so adored!

JUDITH

Hast thou seen my father, Thomas Quiney?

I am bade 'gainst my will to meet him home.

QUINEY

I care not for thy father's whereabouts,

but welcome thy warm presence hereabouts.

JUDITH

I tire of thy false flatteries, sirrah.

Hast thou seen my father William Shakespeare?

QUINEY

If I had, I would blot it out of mind.

JUDITH

If it were but so simply done for me.

As it is, I must have missed his coming.

QUINEY

Dost thou admire my jerkin, Miss Shakespeare?

JUDITH

Thou dost jerk thy jerkin, if thou thinkest

That I care for thy vulgar covering!

QUINEY

Thou dost smother me with what I love best.

JUDITH

What is that, sirrah?

QUINEY Why nothing more than barbéd wit!

JUDITH

Then thou wouldst be killed with loving malice.

QUINEY

Aye, and die within thy murd'rous eyes.

JUDITH

Then Thomas, I am for thee after all!
For I wouldst mar all thy mistreadings base,
With misery and break thy pate with hate.
Yet methinks that not e'en thy affection
For flagellation wouldst endure my love
Of sharpéd spite. For thy own benefit,
My spaniel dear that loves a kicking hard,
Find gentler lover and a safe mistress,
Then leave me to my dark and mournful mischief.

QUINEY

Wait.

JUDITH Thou dost seem to enjoy inflicting
Pain as much as receiving it in kind!

QUINEY

If thou wilt receive my inflictéd pain,
I will morph it into sensuous pleasure.
An alchemist of feeling thus am I,
Transforming one sensation to another.

JUDITH

It wouldst be a true scientist who could
Philos'pher's stone so use to transform my grief.
Dost thou truly think thou canst turn this heart,
So full of iron dross, to purified gold?

QUINEY

Iron is tougher stuff than yellow gold.

JUDITH

But less supple, so I say once again,
I am not for thee, despite thy attempts,
Which have been many these past sev'ral years.

QUINEY

Doth that not speak to my bold constancy?

JUDITH

It doth speak to thy bold stupidity.

QUINEY

Wilt thou receive not my sweet love nor hate,
But give me such lukewarm indifference?

JUDITH Indifference! Then let me be clear, thou lewd, dankish coxcomb: I have had enough of thy coy, cowish coverture! Thy beslubbering words are a pox and a plague on my life, and I will no longer be beholden to such blazoned, blubbering bibble-babble! I do entreat thee that thou shouldst inflict such posturing pestilence into some other woman's ear, for I will not submit to such venomous poison! I wouldst have nothing to do with such a fen-sucked, quarrelsome, quat of a sheep-rump!

QUINEY

O, I'm enrapturéd and ravishèd!
Poet of hard love, soft hate, speak again!
Speak again!

JUDITH

Most despicable, impossible rogue!

Exit Judith.

QUINEY

What passion full of flame and fiery fury!
Nay, she is not indifferent, indeed!
I do thus spy some marks of hate within her,
And if she hates me, then, betimes, she'll love me.
Dost not follow such arithmetic?
Then I shall prove my answer by and by.
Beholdest in my cunning, keen, design
An art far 'yond of Fake-speare, shalt thou find.

Exit Quiney.

*

~ I.2 *"New Place," Stratford-upon-Avon, the Shakespeares' home. ANNE HATHAWAY SHAKESPEARE and SUSANNA SHAKESPEARE are preparing the house. Enter Judith.*

JUDITH

I was unable to locate him, Mother.
Nowhere could I find him at the gates.

ANNE

I did remind thee of thy tardiness.

SUSANNA

If thou didst miss our Father at the gates
Why is he not met here before thee thus?

ANNE

His rambling, stumbling feet; at best know not
Straight ways, but wander as a bee to hive.
'Tis ready all?

SUSANNA Aye, Mother, that I'll warrant
the critic-stranger would, amazed, proclaim,
"Thy house is clean and bright as courtesy!"

ANNE

'Tis not made for strangers, but thy father.

JUDITH

Is diff'rence to be had?

SUSANNA Be not so saucy,
'Tis not becoming to a gracious lady.

JUDITH

Lady! Judith Shakespeare coarse and plain!
Thou hast swallowéd whole myths, Susanna;
I am no more a lady than that portrait,
Whose lady fine is preening over there.

SUSANNA

Thou art a gentle's daughter, that is true.

JUDITH

I am the seed of a knavish, bawdy actor;
An upstart poet who had high ambitions
That vaulted him straight o'er these guarded walls!

ANNE

That coat of arms would quarrel with thee, miss,
On that point, methinks.

JUDITH Forsooth, coat of arms!

Bedeviléd, pretending coat of arms
Should's marry this false portrait of a lady,
And cry themselves honoréd gentry then!
Inanimate, the pairéd lord and lady
May advance to King James's court, forthwith,
And scrape the floor, if they behave well 'nough.

ANNE

Why this sour disposition today?
I'd so love to see thee bonny-happy.

JUDITH

I would see us all thus happy, Mother,
If father were here to make it rightly so.

ANNE

He shall be here today and make thee seer.

JUDITH

Once here, then gone again; so swift and slippery,

Thus trav'ling as a bouncing, speedy stream.

ANNE

Nay, what thou dost cozen is thy father's substance.

JUDITH

Then why doth he run wet 'tween my fingers
When I try to keep him?

ANNE Berate him still?

'Tis his so gen'rous hand that hath provided
Our Home, New Place, this grand roof overhead

JUDITH

Yet his so gen'rous head sleeps rarely here.

SUSANNA

He oft provided home for us in London.

JUDITH

Which home, the Globe so great or the Blackfriars?
Confess, I liked both houses well enough,
But found no bed in them to call my own.

SUSANNA

Thou lookest not in Father's warméd heart,
For there I've always found a goodly rest.

JUDITH

Aye, for thou art thus his favorite child,
Susanna, loved, so like his dear Cordelia.

SUSANNA

If any favor is thus given me,
It is because I have provided rest.
Cold winds shan't bite his tirèd, weary face

JUDITH

Here trav'lers should expect the wind and ice,
So thus ask not sweet breath nor warmth from me.
What needs that man my love, that knave my praise,

When he doth have his approbation 'ready
From clucking groundlings, and King's court alike,
Their hands and voices raised in cheers, loud
shouts?
O, if he only didst need less from those
Who doth not now, not then, know his blind heart.
But, rather, if he yearned for those who 'wait
His absent steps to reach our welcome door,
If he didst give horse rest within our stables,
And bring a comfort to our dame's best bed,
Then wouldst thou see brash youth spin and grow
old,
And find my words grow warm to cast out cold.

ANNE

I bespeak thee sternly, shrewish daughter.
Is this the baleful token thou presents
In gratitude for Father's generous heart?
Nay, Judith, thou shalt not so leave it thus,
'Til thou shalt then deliver honest answer!

JUDITH

Why do you, Woman, shrive his by-past sins,
Thou who art most offended by neglect?

ANNE

Speak'st hist'ry as a scholar well-acquainted!
As if a child, how wantonly thou brayest.
I thought that I had raised thee to the height
Of handsome gentlewoman, and fair born
But thou dost still thy faerie stories prattle
Of airy creeds of brash and naive, nymphs.
There be reasons for the desolation,
Ruìn, and wrack of my hoped for bride's bed.

Thy judgment rash doth not shepherd these gre
Dark, secrets into her short estimation.
Fulsome art thou in thy ign'rance of
The wide world, floating bitter fancy 'bout thee,
Flashing flesh of thy fair, fav'rite fables.
In that, thou art thy father's daughter true!

JUDITH

Nay, his parenting was thus spent abroad.
As thou say'st, I am but ignorant.
Yet how then didst thou and the Will of Words
So raise a rough and dim benighted daughter?
Unlike thee and the nobler Susanne,
I cannot even scratch out my own name

Exit Judith.

SUSANNA

If she were mine, I would slap her fresh face.

ANNE

Dost thou now also rudely upbraid me?

SUSANNA

Nay, I would see the brightest archangels
Bring thee manna-like comfort at all times.
Thou didst accost her impudence most bravely.

ANNE

But in so doing, did I lose her love?

SUSANNA

What is a child's love, if used as a scepter
To reign with most base, selfish tyranny?

ANNE

Yet I long for such, even if I am
Made subject to its stern looks once awhile.

ANNE

Yet I long for such, even if I am
Made subject to its stern looks once awhile.

SUSANNA

Say not so, for thou hast this child's sweet love,
With some to spare.

Enter William.

ANNE

Grateful, which I am, for that good spare
I may yet need to use up. Here he comes.

SUSANNA

Papa!

WILLIAM Delight of my affections, true,
She who waits for me, thus ever faithful,
She who never doubts my heart to be true!

SUSANNA

Delight is mine, today, my dearest Papa.
Like Spring, you bless me with thy safe return
That blasts the frost! With frigid binding winds.
Cold gone, I smell but sweetest apple blossoms.

WILLIAM

O how I revel in thy words!

ANNE Husband.

WILLIAM

Good morrow, good Anne.

ANNE Thou callest me good,
good Will?

WILLIAM

Always good. That be not doubted, never.

ANNE

In faith, I thought it doubted thus, ever.

WILLIAM

I am in good spirits. Let us leave it.

ANNE

If thou say'st so, Husband.

WILLIAM So, I say it.

Aye, in gentle earnestness I say it.

ANNE

Gentle spirits, indeed!

(Aside:)

How comes all this?

In so few visits a year, 'tis rare thing
For him to seem content or peaceful here.
Always restless, always ready to go
Back to his wider Globe. Is it thus now?

(To William:)

The house-is finished, anon. Should I also
Instruct the cook to put the fire on?

WILLIAM

I am not hungry, Anne, but for one thing.

ANNE

What one thing is that?

WILLIAM Nothing.

ANNE Say nothing?

Dost thou jest with me?

WILLIAM If I do so jest,

I shall take the trickster Puck's joke further.

SUSANNA

This levity lewd, I find, is not for me!

Exit Susanna. William kisses Anne.

ANNE

Will, thou art in a rare mood.

WILLIAM Why so rare

For man to want to kiss his fairest friend?

ANNE

Do not mock me, sir.

WILLIAM In faith, I do not.

ANNE

I wouldst almost think I have met thy twin,
Like those mistaken in thy comedies.

WILLIAM

By my troth, this is no Com'dy's error.
Anne, I would like to make thee laugh—loudly.

ANNE

If this be no jade's trick, and belikest thou
To finish this wet race, then I say we ought
Take merriment unto another quarter.

WILLIAM

Aye, so that we may roll in won'drous laughter.

Exeunt.

*

~ I.3 *Enter Judith, carrying a small portrait.*

JUDITH

I spy this bright, beaut'ous portrait again.
A stray witness wouldst think I pine for one
That I could call my love, or such, divine
Of heart, of hand, of soul, in short, a man
But this be not a man, nor 'tis a woman,

Unless you think I'm bent towards that wild wind.
Nay, this figure that sits beside me in
This painting small and dear to my slight heart,
'Tis not a man, but couldst have been if he'd
been granted longer, loving life to live.
All revealèd, it is Hamnet, my twin,
My poor, dear brother, dead, so long gone now.
He wast but ten and one, so I the same,
When Hades claimed his spirit soft and small.
Was Death was so cruel, to not bring me with him?
What man or woman e'er could fill the ache
Left by him whom with me shared tender womb?
Not all soul mates are made after the shape
of wild-hearted lovers made so passionate.

(Enter Hamnet's Ghost.)

What small boy is this belooks so cold?
'Tis truly thee? Oh, what a vision is this!
Say hap'ly so! If I blench at this sight,
Will he leave me? Depart not, spirit dear!
Hamnet! Hast thou words for me? Speak now.
A mute ghost he appears, but frightful not.
Sweet boy! dost thou not even recognize me?
I am much changèd since we last embraced.

HAMNET Joy.

JUDITH

He speaks, if only but a single word.
Yes, boy, my warm face touch, if thou art real.
I can't feel fingers, 'though I see them there.
I did but now our childhood portrait view.
My wits, have they now fled my grievéd mind?
Care I if it was provéd even so?

Nay, I delight in this bright youthful, ghost,
I would have him always in my view.
What bringsest thee from shadowed purgatory?
Nay, not from that contested, wracked, dim place!
Thou wast but a pure child, thy heart of bliss,
Hence from a heaven art permitted thus,
As Hermes brings a message. Is that so?

Enter William, unseen by Judith.

HAMNET Joy.

Exit Hamnet.

JUDITH

Please, do not leave me so unsatisfied!
How fleet and short thou art, oh joyous herald.
But since thy brief, bright light extinguishèd,
The previous dark I am made more aware.

WILLIAM

Who was that boy thou didst speak to just now?

JUDITH

Father! Didst thou see him?

WILLIAM Nay, not his face,

Thou didst obscure that. He reminded me
Of one poor boy I knew who came to me
In manner so the same.

JUDITH Thou art confused.

This boy, he was a stranger to thy face.

WILLIAM

Perhaps as thy acquaintances, thy griefs,
Are thus known to me much more intimate
Than thou hast e'er considered. Other matters:
Proclaims thy mother of thy anger hot.
Dost thou have a quarrel with me, Judith?

JUDITH

My feelings for thee have ever been constant
Since I was a child: Thou dost boil my blood.

WILLIAM

Thy answer is but brutal honesty.
Know'st thou how often thou art in my thoughts?

JUDITH

Thy thoughts may breed and copulate forever,
But they send no child, boy nor girl, to me.

WILLIAM

My thoughts are not my children true; thou art.

JUDITH

Think so in truth? Nay. O how thou liest;
For see how thoughts have taken up dire flesh
And formed to strut and dance and die again
Only to be resurrected anew.
Are these not thy brave brood in very deed?

WILLIAM

Aye, I do love those, playing, happy shadows.
Yet I love not the shadows for themselves,
But for the 'membered forms in which I cast them
Hast thou not seen thy copy dear in them?

JUDITH

What, sayest thou? I walk in Regan's gait;
That Gon'ril's serpent tooth I bravely wear?

WILLIAM

Nay, thou art my Viola, dearest twin
That didst survive the storm, but die in heart
To see her brother dear sink 'neath the waves.
Dost thou believe, thy father's poor eyes can
But see in thee the joy he saw in him?

For when thou lost thy noblest, sweetest twin
So did I feel the wrack myself herein.
He was my son;
And thou art my dear daughter.

JUDITH And yet thou wast not there when we saw his life fall away.

Exit Judith.

WILLIAM

Aye, like thy broken heart, that pains me still.

Enter Anne.

ANNE How dost thou, Will?

WILLIAM Thou didst speak aright. She hateth me.

ANNE

Thou didst think once I hated thee with spite;
That with my hate I threw thee straight away;
That hate was but short-sighted counterfeit.
It couldst not last, for I do know thy heart.

WILLIAM

But she knows not my heart, my mind, thou dost,
That is the chiefest wound at root herein.
I did so many summers tell her this,
"I am thy father true, thy chiefest kin,"
Then fell away like dead and yellow leaf,
Once green when air was warm and wise and wholesome,
Grown brittle now, when the winter air doth sting.

ANNE

The storms have now returned to thy grim brow,
Thou didst arrive so full of joyous cheer.
I hoped that such bright sunshine last anon,
But here thy somber thoughts, are all in mourning.

Didst thou not come in colored glad, array
With full intent to thus enjoy the day?

WILLIAM

Aye, such was my sincere intent to do.
As I was on my journey home today
I thought of bitter nights, how far they seemed.
From this green land I once was banishéd
And am now called the town's great father, good.
I am now hailed a gentleman rich and true;
And rich I am, so 'tis not without right!
I purchaséd that coat of arms to show
What father did, and what he failed to do,
Now lives in me as prophecy fulfilled.
'Tis boastful joy to finally claim glad honor?
Such wealth, such hope, such bliss, such happiness?
And e'en when I saw thee, who suffered most
My absence as a hardened accusation,
And turned against thy heart and blessed honor,
Which honor made me suffer in return,
I did not see our pains and arguments,
Instead remembered I the day I saw
Thy darling face gaze warm at me in full
And I remembered: I did truly love thee.

ANNE

Hold to, dearest husband, and keep such love
Within thy breast that it may stay contained.

WILLIAM

When I saw this warm land I lingered so
That comfort did light on my welcomed finger,
Like bird in gayest confidence doth dare
To trust a giant to its tender care,

But move with slightest tremor and thus see
That brav'ry gone, flown back to angry sea.

ANNE

Will, where goest thou?

WILLIAM Alas, I tire,

And thus will I follow suit and then retire.

Exit William.

ANNE

Exquisite bliss and plaguéd heart did ne'er
In such close quarters live as now do mine.
I urged him marry me when child conceived,
In hopes the love I saw in him would last,
But now e'en after all these lonely years,
His mind still rounds and turns to former tears.

Enter Susanna.

SUSANNA

Dear Mother, fare thou well?

ANNE I fare fair 'nough.

SUSANNA

Not all is well 'twixt Judith and thy Father.

ANNE

Nay.

SUSANNA And what is betwixt thee and my father?

He seemed so merry before.

ANNE He was. We were.

SUSANNA

And then...?

ANNE The sand hath settled in the water,

And he did thus see me so clear again.
I was no mermaid as imagined before.
A siren, rather.

SUSANNA Nay! Say not thus so.

He loves thee. That I know. It must be true.

ANNE

And by what sign canst I know such more truly?
Before-time I gained tokens of his love
And pledged my faith in those blessed sacraments.
But caught I more sheets of professèd love
With signature of his, to a strange, dark name
Some other lady he must hold more dear.
My pilgrim's prayers were caught in my dry throat,
I felt to curse what I once worshippéd!
But these aren't thoughts for my own darling
daughter.
Bright myths I taught her of eternal love.
A child should trust her parents love each other.

SUSANNA

That is no myth, I've seen it in thee both.
For I desire to see such fire re-kindled.
My eyes lied not, they saw great love betwixt thee,
Nor lied thy honest hearts

ANNE Believe it still.

Perhaps thy faith shall purge dark heresy.
But I am now exhausted, tired, worn, and whittled
by the long day.

Exit Anne. Enter William, unseen.

SUSANNA

O what little hope this all gives to me,
When I see love stripped from those who claimed it
In their younger days of morning sunlight,
When their hearts were light as was their conscience.
Look how weary with sin and grief they are

Now that youth and vitality are gone.
Look at how tired and dark their eyes draw down
To the mournful earth that calls them down
Give their regrets up to her slumber.
Doth this love lay down her burden quick,
When opposèd by lethargic fatigue?
Can it rise again, a Lazarus?
I have my own love locked within here
That I dare not utter to evil air,
Hopes like these plucked from our breasts exposed.
This Pandora with her secret box,
Safe as long as I do not unlatch it?
But once love, made plain to the whole, wide world,
Doth she then begin to break down, exposed
This cold, mortal air gives dank, dark chill
Killing not only she, her own dear self
'Twill infect her with a des'prate kiss
Her proclaimèd love, that whole, wide world,
Spores sent from her stinking, cursèd mouth
Into ears who hear her base infections.
Best it is to keep closèd this box,
Love protected, binding it with locks.

Exit Susanna.

WILLIAM

I have heard this and cannot unhear it.
My dear daughter, whom I truly adore
Cannot love another since she believes
Wretched Will, I, cannot love her dear mother.
I, who doth write thus 'bout love so often,
Hath made my Susanna's love a coffin.
My unworthy heart I must thus forswear

And place a better one again in there.

Exit William.

Belinda Purdum as Susanna Shakespeare (foreground) and Zel Bromley as Judith Shakespeare (background). Photo by Emily Drew

Belinda Purdum as Susanna Shakespeare.
Photo by Brian Randall.

Belinda Purdum as Susanna Shakespeare
and Zel Bromley as Judith Shakespeare.
Photo by Brian Randall.

Sam Schofield as Thomas Quiney and Bradley Moss as William Shakespeare. Photo by Emily Drew.

*

~ II.1 *Outside New Place. Enter Judith and Quiney.*

JJUDITH

What must I do to thus be rid of thee?

QUINEY

Just Marry me; then all is as should be,

Done, no reason I'd find to thus tarry,

'Cept meals, prayérs, and when we make merry.

JUDITH

And look, here's my house, thou art forbidden.

QUINEY

How so, there be some enchantment hidden?

Perhaps there is some witch's charm or hex?

JUDITH

Magic that makes your ships into mad wrecks.

QUINEY

Then thou dost not know the powers of rhyme

That makes thee mine, if I but bide my time.

JUDITH

Nay, tardy clocks tell erroneous hours,

And truants shall be locked, put out our tow'rs!

QUINEY

Judith, just listen!

JUDITH

Get thee gone, Thomas!

Exit Judith.

QUINEY

(Aside:)

Thou might call me a fool to thus persist,

But her sweet witch's charms I can't resist.

Enter WILLIAM.

WILLIAM

Who is this tree that plants in front my house?

QUINEY

Thou dost know me.

WILLIAM

Pray, I do not, sirrah.

QUINEY

Thou knowest me! Mock me not, base Shakespeare!

WILLIAM

Know thee? By what should I know thee, Quiney?

QUINEY

Thou dost now confess it!

WILLIAM

Nay, deny it!

To know thee, thou wouldst need be noteworthy.
Thy father, I knew him, he wast good man.
This mewling whelp, though, mule's back bottom,
He, I have quickly thus forgotten.

QUINEY

I am thus known! A vinter, tobacc'nist,
A man and merchant, master of many!
Thus learned, I, *maîtriser de les Français;*
I do thus more than scribbles, scrying scrapes!
A Mule? Not I. Thou art the ass on stage:
Thus belching flat'lent fancies that add not
To our community's good benefit!

WILLIAM

Pardon me, this is purposeless matter.
Better I knew than to engage with thee.

QUINEY

O 'zounds, master of words cannot retort?

WILLIAM

Let us, sir, bury our useless malice,
Instead, come, I offer thee my chalice.

QUINEY

O calm dishonor, vilest submission!
Not worthy thy feigned, fainting, feckless fame,
Thy foul fortune made thus effeminate
By base and hermaphrodite origin!

WILLIAM

Take care, thou brash and brainless, beardless youth,
Thou dost not desire me an enemy...

QUINEY

That is precisely my deep desire! Youth!
I am a man, a beard as full as thine!
Accosts thou well on stage's protection,
Where swords are blunted, faux finis thus writ,
Thy false and vain, constructed victory,
But how dost thou fare when the blood is real
And knives are sharpened?

WILLIAM How can I not laugh!

I've tried to publish peace, but O now this!
Thou speakest as if thou art worldly thus?
A large, strong wrestler riding our world's stage?
I stood before our Gloriana, Queen,
Receivéd her blessed, standing applause.
I've crossed my wits with wickedest, wild Wits!
E'en after noble Christopher Marlowe
Fell mysteriously in a little room,
I survived enemies and critics, all;

When Kit could no more deliver his speech,
I continued with my soliloquies.
Essex's Earl, to rebel, used my play
Against the Queen, to commit high treason!
Yet when his head fell, my cool wit stood tall.
Thou thinks the blade thou boasts of is sharp?
Thus try the basest blade stabbed Kit's poor heart,
Or ax that sliced through Essex Earl's weak neck!
Where they fell, I was standing, tall and sure!
I have thus scolded our dread, Scottish king,
And publicly bewitched his occult fears!
And still he invited me to his court,
Our blesséd patron, His crown our Comp'ny's
stamp.
When Ben Jonson was thrown in dark prisons,
Here I was invited to 'grave my name
To James's translation of Holy Writ.
My plays read, thou shalt see my travels wide:
To France and culture's seat, great Italy!
Thus, I traversed a globe beyond my Globe,
I basked in bishops', monarchs' majesty,
I have seen rebellions, tempests, and plagues,
By God's good grace, I lived to tell my tales.
Thus, ask me not to heed quaint arrogance.
Thou wantest to take aim at Mighty Man,
Yet empty quips, conceited sentences,
Thy frantic, paper bullets of the brain,
The salt of the earth still hath its savor,
But thy boasts stand little in my favor.

QUINEY

Shouldst I now bow, O great, mighty Shakespeare?

WILLIAM

Nay, instead let us humbly strike a peace.
Thou hast hot pepper with thy hearty salt,
Would I rather find reasons for our love
To grow, than noxious weeds of basest hate.

QUINEY

Have I but one reason to thee thus love,
And a legion reasons to thee thus hate;
Thus, mark me, I shall cut that one reason
From out thy rotting, black plaguéd carcass,
And I shall take her, make her sweetly mine,
Then I shall leave thy corpse to fester, rot,
A monument to laughing folly, thine.

WILLIAM

Her?

QUINEY

How little carest thou for thine own fields,
As thou dost wander about thy fair Globe!
Give heed to wisest word of man who plows,
Ignoréd fields are eaten by the cows.

Exit Thomas.

WILLIAM

(Aside:)

O why doth this man shake my confidence,
As if the critics of my youth had strength
To banish me from Stratford once again?
Like that poached deer I slew those years long past,
I freeze in fear under the hunter's glare.

(Voices are heard.)

Yet hear I bestirring of voices loud!
I must awake from this too potent spell.
It is my daughter Susannah and, why,
That is John Hall the honored physician.
In good faith, truly respectable man.
Is it thus he whom she set her dear love?
I must hear this, so shall hide in casement.

William hides. Enter Susanna and John Hall.

JOHN

Beloved Susannah, wait!

SUSANNA Sir, I cannot!

JOHN

Nay, tarry but a short while and explain
Why thou hast violently torn our love
When it was fair and valued by you once,
as thou confessed so oft to me before.
I pray thee, tell what perfidious star
Hath struck and drained the bright, wholesome verdure
Of love, now rain run out high Welkin's cheek.

SUSANNA

Nay, I cannot! But since thy sad eyes wear
Such mournful expression, know that 'tis not
by fault of thine. Thou art the bright zenith of
Admiration, still idol of my heart.
But I cannot say more lest I injure
My own firm purpose! John, we must not wed!

WILLIAM

(Aside:)

Should I now speak at this and interfere?
My daughter tells of my damned fool's mishaps

And my deeds need not be her dowry dire?

JOHN

Not wed? Thou mayest as well say be dead!
For that is what shall occur to my heart
If we depart from here thus twain.

SUSANNA   Say not,

But be content that we met with true love,
Its sweetest taste pollen like bees to buds,
This cargo fraughting to our hives, our hearts,
Before the fresh and fragrant flow'rs wilted
And died. Instants of love are nigh better
Than to thus see love turn to endless hate.

JOHN

Why speak of love's death, morphed thus into hate?
What betid thy poor mind and infected
thee with such notions sad?

SUSANNA   I can say naught...

WILLIAM

(Aside:)

I cannot let this be.

SUSANNA

...Just we are done.

WILLIAM

(Aside:)

I have now concocted artifice keen!
I'll prove and manifest their truest love.
There be no sharper spur to swift action
Than oppose, pause for burnéd reaction

William reveals himself.

SUSANNA

O Father!

WILLIAM

Aye, daughter, though thy secrets
Exposed show base betrayal 'gainst my will!

SUSANNA

In what possible way have I transgressed?

WILLIAM

Thou didst transcend thy family's conflict
'Tween my dear parent's cherished Cath'lic faith,
And former Queen's 'forcement of her father's
Adulteries most vainly justified.
Thou hast gone to a worst, pitched party third,
Thou hast tied thyself to a Puritan,
The overbearing, inveterate foe of
My house, aye, my whole belovéd Globe!

JOHN

Dear sir, ere thou condemn me for my faith,
List how a Puritan loves thy daughter
Thus purely.

WILLIAM Nay, I shan't take poison that
Would place all dearest things I love to mort!
I submitted my humors to thy care,
But surgeon's knife shall not touch my daughter!

SUSANNA

O Father, thou art livid, hot today,
Allow thy gentler nature have more sway!

WILLIAM

Speak not for him, deserves he not thy love.

SUSANNA

A more deserving man I have not met!

WILLIAM

Thy experience with men is thus too short!

This man is not thus comely, wise, nor good,
To hold so fast to a cruel religion.

JOHN

No, sir, it's thy words, not my faith that shows
A judging disposition and heart cruel

WILLIAM

Dost thou think so? Thou art a scurvy fool,
In addition to thy other base faults.
Thou hast not worn the actor's reviled cap!
In London, it is Puritan complaint
That hath set laws against the player's craft
Banished us from city to the outskirts,
A broken barge tossed on unmannéd isle.
'Tis thy people's self-righteous preachings, cruel,
That caused the Master over Revels to
Take censor's pen, nay, his sharp, deadly sword,
And wound my plays and lame their arms with cuts
That they are blunted thus in their battles!
E'en out of city Puritans offend,
For when we are on tour it hath been thy
Poxed Puritan Councils that barréd us
Entrance to towns and quite a many shires,
Where we eke out living in times of plague.
E'en our dear Stratford lists to Puritans,
So that I never found the honor dear
In my own country, elsewhere obtainéd.
Thus, my own children were barred meanly from
The sight of their own father's art 'mong peers
'Twas not 'til came they to my London stage
That viewed they visions that I made for them

SUSANNA

No, thou gives this man baseless injury.
When thou doth lay such fault at his pure feet,
Who took no part in wrongs to thy good art.

WILLIAM

A Puritan, is he not?

JOHN Ay.

WILLIAM Then so.

SUSANNA

Not so! Hath not a Puritan conscience?
O, wrong or right, they live by their own light.
As thou dost say what thou wilt in thy plays,
Despite the cons'quence it for others means.
So doth a Puritan claim his right to,
according to his own mind, influence.
Still, see not this man by another's light,
E'en those of his own faith, fam'ly, or tribe.
I beseech thee, see this man by his heart,
Individual in its sphere and part.

WILLIAM

Susann, thou art fair minded Portia, mine,
'Cept thou didst take the poor foreigner's part,
Shown mercy, even a dear, truest love
To the cold stranger within our closed gates.
Shylock is well represented by thee,
Thou wouldst have shown the Jew's humanity.

SUSANNA

Then thou dost approve of his marriage suit?

WILLIAM

Aye, but last I spied, there was another
Last barrier and wall had he to scale.

SUSANNA

I near forgot; I cannot marry him...
Or so I thought.

JOHN
Thou art undone, my love,
Methinks, by father's keen's uncanny wit.

SUSANNA
Aye, he hath shown the glaring folly of
My frightened argument. Forswear, I will,
From comparing my love with another's
Scales crafted by another's state,
And be a maker of my own love's fate

Susanna and John kiss.

WILLIAM
Now come, good Master Hall, enjoy our hall,
And our good fam'ly's courtesy and fire,
That we may thus become familiar.
Dost thou play chess? We are a gaming sort.

JOHN
Aye, but the kind of chess Susann and I
engage in has even more playful sport.

SUSANNA
Remember that he is my father, John!

WILLIAM
Thou needst not fear, I was young once as well.

Exit William, Susanna, and John.

*

~ II.2 *Inside New Place. There are the sounds of reveling in the next, unseen room. Enter William with an empty serving dish to be filled. He stops and weeps. Enter Anne.*

ANNE

Husband, art thou not well on joyous day?

WILLIAM

Leave me, I will attend to thee there soon.

ANNE

I've left thee be, near our whole long marriage;
Wilt thou not ope thy mind to me e'en on
Our dear, sweet daughter's wedding feast, Will'iam?
I wish to aid thy heart.

WILLIAM I do not doubt.

Thou wast woven with tender stuff, dear Anne.

ANNE

Indeed, if I am dear to thee, then speak.

WILLIAM

How speak when my heart has no tongue to voice?

ANNE

Let thy heart write, 'haps it just needs a quill.

WILLIAM

My heart is oft a solitary thing,
Shy to tenderest touch.

ANNE

Shy thou hast been.
Thou hast been willing to play the brash clown
On stage, but then withdraw when thou doth step
Off of the planks and 'mongst mortals again.
Learn from women: What you thus think, do speak.

WILLIAM

Thou stole that from me.

ANNE

What, you ne'er borrowed
From Kit Marlowe, or Thomas Kyd?

WILLIAM

Ay, Ay,

Cannot I hide from thee? If I to war
went, thou wouldst still find me and wag thy
tongue!

ANNE

Ay, I am yet a persistent lover.
But, Will, why hide? Why not come home for good?

WILLIAM

And abandon London, our rich living?

ANNE

Look about thee! Thou art rich already!
What need thee of more plays or more players?
We have gallant New Place o'er our good heads,
Plenty of gold safe, tucked, ready in store,
Thy clever wife hath taken care of our
Investments that have multiplied talents,
Making a rich man a very rich man.
Done well, is not? Art thou thus not free now?

WILLIAM

Canst lonely men ever truly be free?

ANNE

What loneliness shouldst thou hold with me near?
Is not a loyal wife comfort enough?

WILLIAM

Hast thou been loyal, true, and chaste always,
With me so oft conveniently away?

ANNE

Hath thy green-eyed jealousy now returned?
Thou saidst that those accusations were cold.
That sin thou cleared of fair Desdemona,

Thus, I thought thou didst shrive its base, false pitch
From thy mind darkened and my innocence!
I have been thy true companion, e'en when
Thou hast not been true to our lonely bed!

WILLIAM

Broken sacred wedding vows, have I not,
Save for when I thought thou didst break that trust!

ANNE

E'en if that were verily true as bond,
Of which I have oft had dark, broken doubts,
Canst thy wand'ring eyes, thoughts, and pen say so?
Or is this Dark Lady in thy sonnets
As mythical as wild Titania?

WILLIAM

Those were published without my permission!

ANNE

But yet they shouted thy perversities
From the very housetops! The shame they caused!

WILLIAM

Thou dost not perceive their significance,
Nor the truest meaning of my poor heart.
Thou dost know that many were writ for thee!

Enter Susanna, in her wedding clothes.

SUSANNA

Father, Mother, thou dost a Babel make!
So much that e'en if Will Kemp's ghost were here
He would not laugh.

WILLIAM

Meant not to disturb guests,
We beseech thy pardon, dear Susanna.

I cursed; Thy mother dropped the pudding black.

ANNE

And then thy father broke pitcher and plate,
Thus, fell down on his ass and hurt his pate!

Exit Anne.

SUSANNA

Fair omen, this is not, my dear Father,
Do I see my future writ by thy din?
Do fair loves all begin as this day,
Only to fall into harsh disarray?

WILLIAM

O come hither, daughter, lend me thy hand.

Susannah gives her palm to William. He reads it.

SUSANNA

What dost thou, my Papa, is this some game?
It will take more than old gambols to free
Me from the crows that hover near our feast.

WILLIAM

This be an old trick I did learn from some
Three crones who taught me their myster'ous art.
Within thy blessed palm resides thy future.
This here is thy heart line. Since Nuptial Day,
Let us begin thus there, scry thy fortunes
In love.

SUSANNA

Wrinkle not so thy brow! What is revealed?

WILLIAM

O my dear girl, thou art blesséd and true!
The line is long, to the index finger.
With thy man thou shalt rest in loving bliss.

SUSANNA

'Tis so? 'Tis so! I mean, a merry jest.

WILLIAM

Thy mind line as I would have fairly hoped
Thy education was thus catered to
Thy thirst for knowledge. Judith had other
Claims to her time, though no less observant.

SUSANNA

Aye, she is sharp.

WILLIAM But thy line more steady.

Thy life line...

SUSANNA O tell me not that, forbid!

No soul desires to know that in advance!

WILLIAM

Life lines tell quality of the journey,
Not length of life.

SUSANNA O then pursue the course.

WILLIAM

Thou hast a semi-circle, long and deep.
Which signifies thy health, vitality.
A vibrant living thou shalt surely have.

SUSANNA

I do have cheery hands!

WILLIAM Yet do Forbear,

Let us see what lies in thy fate line there.

SUSANNA

A line of Fate? That doth sound ominous.
The three witches of fate are fickle hags,
And I would not their single eye hover
O'er my poor life.

WILLIAM And they shan't. Thou art free.

I see only their light touch, the rest ruled
by thee, except this cross to thy life line
Which signifies the warm help of fam'ly.

SUSANNA

That I do most humbly welcome with cheer!

WILLIAM

In addition to thy dowry, I give
That gift good fortune writ on thy fair palms.
If I could truly but give thee something
To recompense thy constant love to me.
For I wept in here 'fore thou didst come in,
Berating my constant absence from thee.
I found in thee a joy in my long line,
But I have added many a sorrow,
Yesterday gone, now just the morrow.

SUSANNA

Thou art here now. That is a joy itself,
To have thee here at my brightest moment.

Enter John.

JOHN

I do prithee, Susann, didst thou wed me,
Or thy father?

SUSANNA

Art thou jealous so soon?

WILLIAM

I pray, forgive froward galiant his care
And impatience. I, too, was a brash swain
Turned husband once, and showed my own fair
share
Of ill-favored heat and impertinence.
We are made of weak stuff, each all around.

JOHN

Ay, I do lief correct myself sharply.
I was vexed not at thee, but lack of thee,
and thy dearest, winsome orbit.

SUSANNA Alack,

I thought I lost thy gentleness 'ready,
But now, too true, I see there is naught to
Correct.

WILLIAM

Believe that not a bit. Be wise.

SUSANNA

First I'm too harsh and then too light? How thou
Dost whip me around so to hurt my neck!

WILLIAM

Thus is marriage!

JOHN

Surely, dost thou not take
Such a dim view of holy rites and bliss?

WILLIAM

Real expectation is not dim, but bright.
It is what shall give love its truest light.
I, thy Polonius shall sagely play,
If to thy father's words heed thou shalt pay.

SUSANNA

Too soon to bore us on our wedding day!

WILLIAM

I shall then be brief to such saucy sprites!
And say, sir, that thou art no longer swain,
And, daughter, thy maid's knot to be untied.
'Tis best to cast away the fervent tales
Of perfect love and lovers who err not,

But see across from thee a human form.
In such a face of fault thou shalt then find
A more favoréd meditance to bind.
Rush not to find a stain, nor to berate
But onward move, and clean their dirty slate
Of the wrongs you do so begrudge them there
That love of thine shall rise 'bove ev'ry care.
Now this hypocrite shall go tell my wife
That years past her love saved my worthless life

Exit William.

SUSANNA

Wondrous strange my father, though dear to me.

JOHN

I count myself blesséd, though I be an
Artless fellow, but I find myself in
An artful and resplendent family.

SUSANNA

No, not Artless, nor ever was thus so,
'Though faultless thou may not ever thus be.
Yet it is those imperfections that show
Your most gallant and true humility.
I would not from a portrait of thy face
Hide one odd mole, nor single jarring scar.

JOHN

But doth not wingéd, fancy then doth race
Thy heart to 'magine me by brighter star?
Would it not be better to form me new
Like the clever, clay shaping Pygmalion;
Or Michelangel', who couldst shape God true;
And breathe life in lover-chameleon?

SUSANNA

No such Golem would I make mine so well,
Rather Eve and Adam, though from grace fell.

JOHN

Then if thou wouldst take from my scarlet lips
An imperfect kiss, I would so thee mar.

SUSANNA

Ay, bring those red, twinning cherries thus here.
I will partake of thy forbidden fruit.

Susanna and John kiss.

JOHN

And thus, if fears of thine are now quiet,
Let us show that merry synod our joy
Is not thus so easily abated.

SUSANNA

Let us make Morris jig until we laugh
To our fair marriage bed, to dance anew.

Exeunt.

*

~ III.1 *Inside New Place. Enter Judith followed by Quiney.*

JUDITH

Thy name is not on the guest list, Thomas.

QUINEY

It is not, I confess.

JUDITH

Intruder then,
Upon my sister's most dear assembly!

Belinda Purdum as Susanna Shakespeare and Bradley Moss as William Shakespeare. Photo by Brian Randall.

Bradley Moss as William Shakespeare, Hyrum Stewart as Hamnet Shakespeare, and Zel Bromley as Judith Shakespeare. Photo by Brian Randall.

*Zel Bromley as Judith Shakespeare
and Sam Schofield as Thomas Quiney.
Photo by Emily Drew.*

QUINEY

I would intrude into sacred heaven,
Even if a sulph'rous demon were I,
If such daring brought me closer to thee.

JUDITH

Such fair, sweet words drop from such a foul mouth!

QUINEY

Knowest not my fair mouth. Wilt thou meet it?

JUDITH Nay! I shall not dance this jig with thee, nor engage thy rhythms! Thomas Quiney, thy froward, perverse tongue wouldst make Mephistopheles blush!

QUINEY

Inflict me so, I love cradling curses!
Such ecstasy! I…

Judith hits Quiney-

QUINEY Agh!

JUDITH Art thou in ecstasy now?

QUINEY Why didst thou strike me?

JUDITH Why dost thou speak to me? It is the same to me, as my smackings are to thee.

QUINEY

Nay, my words rough are, but loving in spite.
I do but...

Judith strikes Quiney again.

QUINEY I beseech thee, bate thy hand!

JUDITH What, my hand is as unwelcome as thy lips?

QUINEY My lips do not leave bruises!

JUDITH With how thou didst prattle lustily on, I am

not certain of that!

QUINEY

Thou dost pitch my sad heart in wretched gaol
When thou doth abuse me in such...

Judith strikes Quiney again.

QUINEY Thou art a devil-woman!

JUDITH Ay.

QUINEY Demons wear beautiful faces!

JUDITH Ay! And think of that hell thou wouldst dwell in if I wert thy lover, Thomas Quiney!

QUINEY I can enjoy a little heat...

JUDITH Ay, our passions would be those of fire, but not the kind that thou feelest in thy loins. Rather, it wouldst be the fire that burns thy pate and peels thy skin with unquenchable pain! So, if thou wouldst suffer, court me to thy doom, but if thou wouldst feel relief, be a bachelor!

QUINEY Thou unmuzzled shrew, thou shalt not hear from my suit again!

JUDITH Halloo, Hallay, O happy day!

QUINEY Thou art like thy father! More the fool I to think otherwise!

JUDITH What say ye? I will rip those words from thy offending mouth!

QUINEY The Shakespeares are a cursed kind, a family of vipers! A plague upon thy house!

Exit Quiney.

JUDITH It is quiet. Can it be so? Am I finally rid of that glutton for pain? Such liberty comes unexpected! I should feel joy over the deliverance, but now it seemest to me that I am bootless and utterly alone. Why would I have him back again?

Enter William.

WILLIAM

I was seeking thy distresséd mother,
Only to find my distresséd daughter.
What ails thee, Judith?

JUDITH

Men ail me, Father,
Thus wouldst thy face but make me doubly sick.

WILLIAM

So much distress on such a happy day.

JUDITH

Happy for Susanna, that is not new,
Again she stands on thy tall pedestal,
I am thrown down.

WILLIAM

Who here throws thee thus down?
I wouldst have thee thus stand up in my arms,
Fold thee in my embrace like the bright child
I knew. She had thy eyes, though happ'ier ones.

JUDITH

Aye, they were happy once when they saw thee.

WILLIAM

Why not so now? What guard stands in our way?

JUDITH

The memory and ghost of my brother.

WILLIAM

Would not Hamnet desire thy happiness?

JUDITH

He would.

WILLIAM

I hope for the very same thing.

JUDITH

If I could but believe such happy things.

WILLIAM

Then just believe.

JUDITH Believe...

WILLIAM Is it so hard?

JUDITH

Believe. Believe, aye, then thus be deceived.
Thou dost forget, believed I long ago.
Believed a tale of a Trav'ling, Wise Man,
A myth of a storied, mag'cal wizard.
Told tales of far lands, kings and queens, castles.
This Trav'ling Man brought me many such tales.
A child, thus I loved such bright fantasies,
Now grown, I see them as hypocrisies

Exit Judith. Exit William.

*

~ III.2 *Inside New Place. Anne is onstage, weeping. Enter William.*

ANNE

I thought I was beyond such pebbles wet.
When in our lean, early days we struggled,
I oft was found making these small, damp streams.
And when thou rode to London so far 'way,
I bathed in them without any witness,
Like Artemis, of my own wet skin shy.

Now that I have dared to bathe in them once again,
Hast thou stumbled upon my private place,
And then debased vulnerability.

WILLIAM

Thou art not the virgin, angry huntress.
Thou art my fairest friend, I thy husband.
Thou hast oft exposed thy light, beautous skin
And told me that thou naked wast for me,
And I returned such exposure in same.
Are we now trying to cover all up?
That which we already, intimate know?
Thy tears, to me, are like thy soft caress,
An always welcoméd, bright nakedness.

ANNE

Such fair and faithful words from doubting heart.
I have learnt not to trust their flattery.
Thou dost still yet think me untrue to thee,
Who hath been like an abbess shut away;
Or like a priestess in a Greek temple,
Who only opened holy gates for thee.
Such long days, lonely nights I thus waited
Whilst in London wast thou making fortune...

WILLIAM

A fortune for thee.

ANNE — Ay, ay, which I know.

And after famine, there came sumptuous feast,
Which food thou didst share with us bounteously.
But with that treasure there came steeper price,
We gained a fortune, but lost our crown jewel:
Thy warm company.

WILLIAM — I truly know it,

For as I rode that long, dark, lonely road
Upon my steed t'wards London each cruel Spring,
To put my private thoughts to motley view,
I looked back, and found my heart turned to salt,
Then longing for those loved now left behind:
My fair friend, thou, and our little cherubs.

ANNE

Winters were our haven...

WILLIAM ...No plays performed.

ANNE

I had thee again, to jealously guard.
Greek Persephone's flipped, mirror image:
Sad Demeter's season of grief, our joy.

WILLIAM

Dark Hades was an imperfect husband,
But his heart was true and his sad love ached.

ANNE

Was Persephone thus a captive held,
Or was the underworld heaven misnamed?

WILLIAM

My Anne...

ANNE

No—no! No more poetry, no more sonnets, no more rhythms, no more rhymes, no more flattering illusions and allusions!

WILLIAM

By my troth, Anne, this is my truest heart—

ANNE

'Tis not thy heart I question, but thy feet. Thou art here today, I am able to hold thee in my hands, but tomorrow will bring the storm again that shalt fly thee away! I shall be as Prometheus this time and foresee the fall. This season, it shall be I to fly away!

Exit Anne.

WILLIAM Anne—Anne!

Exit William.

*

~ III.3 *Thomas Quiney's vineyard. Enter Thomas Quiney.*

QUINEY

O wine, tobacco, that is all I need;
To drown and burn myself up 'tis my goal;
Thus I will eradicate my poor heart
Upon the altar of my merchandise.
A woman's womb is not greater than vines,
How much production grows upon it, see!
Thus, Eve's factory's weak matter indeed
Compared to such robust multipliers
And marvelous lusty replenishers!
When set by fruit I grow, women are weak!
As a vintner, I have borne more children
Than whole villages of women with child.
What matters Luna and her mere nine months
When compared to the mighty brood of wine
That hath been borne by my wet art?
By Dionysus' cup, I am fertile!
Dost thou see those tobacco fields o'er there?
Aye, they are mine as well, of my dear wares.
I am a wealthy fellow, loss 'tis hers—
I'm considered an important, great man!

The tobacco yonder there in my fields,
It is more beautiful than any maid.
So lit, its smoke doth make a lusty dance
That seduces better than any wench.
The smoke's sweet kiss, most érotique caress
I prefer to woman's clumsy, crude attempts.
Aye, men may claim that keen desire aroused
From useless rumps, thus false-called fairer sex,
As pinnacle of pleasures physical,
But believe not such miscreant lewdsters!
What need I lumpy, rude feminine kine
When I can feast upon my weeds and wine?

Enter Judith, dressed as a man.

JUDITH I was told by thy man that thou art Thomas Quiney, the master of these purple and green fields.

QUINEY I am that Tom and these are indeed my opulent fields! And who art thou?

JUDITH I am Ganymede Tamson, ever at your service. I operate a tavern in Wilmcote and thus heard such impossible myths of thy wine that I came to either disprove them or partake.

QUINEY Thou art a wine bearer true, dost thou have a cup?

JUDITH Aye, I came thus prepared. Your man sent this with me.

QUINEY Then partake.

Quiney pours and Judith drinks.

JUDITH

Forsooth, thy wine makes me wax rapturous!
Its art and qual'ties art without rival.

QUINEY

Thou singest true the tune of my wet mind,
I just did ponder wine's mightiest worth
Against the poisons that bleed out Eve's teeth.

JUDITH

Ah, thou art wounded too from Eros' point,
Perhaps thou dost need wine's peace more than I.

Quiney drinks.

QUINEY

I thank ye. Thou art strangely prescient.
'Tis true, I am a motley fool for love.
But mistress mine would not be mistress mine,
But rather my ferocious tormentor.
I am an abject monster in her sight,
A thing of wet earth, seaweed, webbéd feet.

JUDITH

And art thou?

QUINEY

Monster, me, do you thus mean?

JUDITH

I know ye not.

QUINEY

I am a creature, 'haps—
A misshaped brute, living in dankest cave;
But if I be a monster, deforméd,
I am a monster that loves a fair maid.

Quiney drinks.

JUDITH

Thou must come off this wine's charms soon enough,
Or thou wilt be a drunken monster, true.

QUINEY

Look, darkness comes so fast upon us now.
Thou spies the moon?

JUDITH

Aye, better seen than thee,
When thy blurred, swimming state is considered.

QUINEY

That moon, it is my friend when I have none.
He shines on me, and comforts me with light
When darkness threatens me with her sharp whip.
When he thus travels to the sky's far side,
I do miss him something quite terrible.

Quiney drinks.

JUDITH

What is that winsome instrument I hear?
It seems to me to come from ev'rywhere
Yet, strangely, also nowhere, all at once.

QUINEY

I've often wondered that very same thing!
I've heard it play, but never found its source.
It is as if thou knowest my mind's text,
The entire book full, past and future writ!
I wish my mistress saw me as thou dost,
Perhaps then she would understand in full.
That haunting instrument doth stir hearts, aye!
It truly makes enchanting melodies.
Is it not wondrous beautiful?

JUDITH 'Tis so.

QUINEY

Ah, moon and music lighten life's burdens.
But, what now, sir, 'tis salt in your sad eyes.

In unpacking my griefs and sorrows felt,
Have I now transferréd them thus to you?

JUDITH

My voice hath left me, now I cannot speak.

QUINEY

Then speakest not, give no noisome prattle.
Sweet silence is oft our best medicine.

JUDITH

I must now depart.

QUINEY Stay.

JUDITH No, I cannot.

JUDITH

My voice hath left me, now I cannot speak.

QUINEY

Then speak not, I need no noisome prattle.
Sweet silence is oft the best medicine.

JUDITH

I must depart, sir.

QUINEY Stay.

JUDITH No, I cannot.

Exit Judith.

QUINEY

Again, abandonéd on my island,
In solitary beauty, thus alone.

Exit Quiney. Re-enter Judith, still dressed as a man.
She goes to the cup, tries to drink from it, but it is empty.

JUDITH

What, treasonous cup, not a drop for me?
It wouldst be so much more the simpler tale

If I could say that he's a vile villain;
Plain dealing, honest villain! I cannot,
As much as I wouldst have it thus so be.
His dark shadow is framed with such bright light,
That I know not what comes from what, or where.
But pity thus the wretch, or marry there,
They are two different things, thus beware:
Following honey, will I find a snare?

Exit Judith.

*

~ IV.1 *The Forest of Arden. Enter Susannah and John.*

SUSANNA

O Mother! Mother!

JOHN Mother Shakespeare! Where!

Susann, art sure of this odd tale told ye?

SUSANNA

The woman, John, was truly in earnest.
She saw my mother here in this Forest.

JOHN

Doth she thus play out Robin Hood's old myths?
Should we play too and be her merry band?
By name's rights, I should then be Little John!
We can get thee some hose and fine doublet
To match hers and make thee young Will Scarlet.

SUSANNA

This is a sober bus'ness, my dear John—

JOHN

Thy father must then cross his sex as well,

He thus must dress the fair Maid Marian.
I'm sure he'd be convincing, verily,
He practiced with dresses and women's shoes
At his rich theatre! What, thou dost laugh?
My Susanna, this be sober bus'ness!

SUSANNA

John, for a Puritan, thou canst be light.

Enter Anne, dressed as a man.

ANNE

But both of thee make terrible outlaws!
With such a din, Nottingham's Sheriff shrewd
Wouldst have sent arrows into both of thee!

SUSANNA

O Mother!

ANNE Nay, I am thy father good.

SUSANNA

Why art thou doing this, my good Mother?

ANNE

No, Father, Father! Have thy ears been stopped?
My wife's play-dreams have so oft aptly proved,
Once I put upon a doublet and hose,
Forsooth, I can now travel, go abroad!
Then forthwith, I am now thy blessed Father,
To travel lands and globe as Will once did
When shackled she was liberated he!

JOHN

Forsooth, there must be laws against all this...

SUSANNA

Dear Mother, why have you abandoned us?

ANNE

Abandoned? Nay, I do as fathers do!

I go forth to traverse and make fortune.
It hath been rare education to see
How differently I am so treated
By constable, by priest, by pauper thus,
When they all see me arrayed like a man.

SUSANNA

Yet in what way did I treat thee diff'rent?
Thou wast always adored by Susanne, yours,
Whether you dressed as woman, or as man.

ANNE

Aye. That is true.

SUSANNA Is that truth not enough?

ANNE

Where is my wife? To London already?

SUSANNA

Nay, he hath delayed until thou art found.
He was just traveling with us anon.

ANNE

Gave up the chase of his reddish roe?
Was she too light, nimble, and quick footed?

SUSANNA

Nay, he hath delayed until thou wast found.
He was just traveling with us anon.

ANNE

Gave up the chase of reddish roe, did he?
Was she too nimble, quick footed, and light?

SUSANNA

Nay, we went one way, he went another.
For thee he searches madly, hunter-like.

ANNE

Aye, hunter, gores he me upon his words

That cut and dig like sharpest arrows, cruel.

SUSANNA

Those words thou once did cherish, I know true,
Thou once read words to me that he writ you.

ANNE

To love such words, 'tis not the same to trust.

JOHN

We come with lanthorn, seek thy care thus out;
But should we pursue this exhausting chase,
When thou desirest not our zealous pace?

ANNE

Aye, listen to thy husband, he hath sense!

SUSANNA

Nay, heed to thy dear husband, he hath love!

ANNE

He lovest not me, but my shadow dark!
When he upon me thinks, he can see bright,
But sun then burns when true me thrust in light!

Enter William.

WILLIAM

Nay, I do love thee, day or in dark night.

ANNE

Thou liest, lovest me thou out of sight!

JOHN

We found her.

WILLIAM

Thank ye. Now unfind us both,
We could use private word betwixt us two.

SUSANNA

Do not let her leave back in this dark wood,
Lest we may never see her face again.

WILLIAM

I won't constrain, nor tie her thus to here,
In truth, she hath now proved herself thus free.

Exit Susanna and John.

ANNE

Thou sayest I am free, such pretty words,
But I have never felt so bound to fate.

WILLIAM

I cannot help what is felt in thy heart,
'Tis burden I cannot carry thus so.

ANNE

I'm strong enough to thus carry my own.

WILLIAM

I do not doubt thy strength, nor courage thine,
Thou hast proved both these many, winding years

ANNE

Then why wouldst I ever need thee? Be gone.
Thou hast proved how irrelevant thou art,
We pushed without thee long these many years.

WILLIAM

I—

ANNE

What, a Will without his Words? A feat!

WILLIAM

Thou hast ripped out my tongue. No words are left.

Exit William.

ANNE

O list to that, how right he is. No words.
It is an abysm I cannot fill...

Silence. Enter Hamnet. Anne struggles with her emotions upon seeing him. She approaches him, hesitant. He is encouraging, with a smile. He shows her the flowers he has been collecting. He first gives her delphinium and points above. She nods. He then gives her statice and points to himself. She nods. He hands her daisies and then points to her. She struggles with this, but then nods. He then hands her myrtle and a rose, and points in the direction that William left. Anne is silent at this, noncommittal. He then hands her lilacs and finally says:

HAMNET Joy.

ANNE struggles with her tears, but then embraces her son.

ANNE

What, Magdala couldst embrace Jesus not,
How is it then that I can embrace thee?

HAMNET Joy.

Enter Judith, still in men's clothing.

JUDITH

O naughty sprite Goodfellow, found again!

HAMNET Joy.

Exit Hamnet.

JJUDITH

Do not leave me again! Nay!

ANNE He is gone.

JUDITH

Thou didst truly see that boy?

ANNE

Aye, thank God.

JUDITH

O blesséd God. I'm not mad after all.

ANNE

Unless we are all Bedlam together.

JUDITH

Has madness become an infectious plague?

ANNE

If so, I would thus die in it.

JUDITH Well said.

This is a marv'lous madness I would keep.

ANNE

I feel I know thee, sir.

JUDITH And I know thee.

ANNE

I don't see how that could be possible,
I am a stranger in this land.

JUDITH So I.

ANNE

Perhaps we're strangers both, wayfaring men,
From far and distant countries traveling,
Then stumble on kinsmen by accident.

JUDITH

Would that not be marvelous?

ANNE Ay, it would.

JUDITH

Well, familiar stranger, God speed ye.

ANNE

But where?

JUDITH Where e'er your heart desires, sir.

ANNE

I am not a sir, but a strong madam!

(Anne takes off her cap and lets her hair run down.)

Exit Anne.

JUDITH

Mother? What madness has come on us all?

Exit Judith.

*

~ IV.2 *Thomas Quiney's Vineyard. Quiney sits in his vineyard. Enter Judith.*

QUINEY

Why, thou art back again! I thought thee lost.

JUDITH

With all thou drank, I am thus sore surprised
Thou dost recall anything from that night.

QUINEY

The moon, my changing receptacle is:
When it is full, I remember it all,
When changes it, my mem'ry's a sliver,
And on the darkest nights, it is all black.

JUDITH

I chanced then upon a full magic night.

QUINEY

Aye, Titania and troupe of fairies bright
Were dancing 'bout.

JUDITH Either that is the tale,

Or Puck dropped flowers into thy sweet ale.

QUINEY

In either case, mad visions were thus had.

JUDITH

I do not doubt thy visions, ecstasy.
Thou drank like Tantalus, now satisfied!

QUINEY

Only to wake to a dry, parchéd throat.

JUDITH

Thou dost still mourn for false, lost Cressida?
Thou art still crossed, sad, pining Troilus then?

QUINEY

Aye, Troilus, he knew women's false, hard hearts!

JUDITH

He knew nothing of women's broken hearts,
As I know not men's mysterious parts.

QUINEY

That is an enigmatic saying, sir.
If I didst not now know thou art a man,
I would say thou dost riddle like a Sphinx.
Alike my love: she's savage, beauty both!

JUDITH

You think her beautiful?

QUINEY Helen's not more!

JUDITH

In what other ways dost thou commend her?
I do but ask academically.

QUINEY

Her wit tears skin, but cleans the whole mind pure,
So that I admire her for abuses.
She shows a keen, bright brain with sharpest words,
I love her all the more for their sweet hurts.

JUDITH

Couldst thou be sincere in such pain seeking?

QUINEY

She doth make pain as exquisite as fire
That burns, but brightens whole, entire rooms.

I wouldst have a single, smart spark from her
Than entire courts of dumb, dull, dim beauties

JUDITH

Go on.

QUINEY Her intelligence is a storm
Of rain that I would stand in all the night
So that I may be drenched in her fair thoughts!

JUDITH

Is she not an injured, wild-eyed creature,
That will claw you if you but approach her?

QUINEY

Her heart is pained, but then so thus is mine,
'haps then we can our harms together wail.

JUDITH

Where is the happiness in all of that?

QUINEY

Happiness may appear diff'rent for us
Who are but half creatures of this dim world.
Our wet skin may reflect sadness thus well
And make it our own unique kind of joy.

JUDITH

What if she's not worthy of such fair thoughts?

QUINEY

She's worthy as thou art.

JUDITH Thou doth know!
How long did I maintain the masquerade?

QUINEY

Dull playmakers think we know not our sex
But I see through such an obvious hex.

JUDITH

O spite! I thought it such a clever ruse!

QUINEY

Perhaps, if thou didst have men's broad shoulders,
And didst eat Adam's lusty apple core.
Why, of a diff'rent color is thy beard
Than that which paints on thy pretty eyebrows!
Not to mention the lumpiness thus made
By thy long, beaut'ous hair beneath that cap.

JUDITH

O my woman's sin is made manifest!

QUINEY

If Eve didst sin, then I will follow her
Out any garden, and into the world.
Without thee paradise is a prison,
That was, we learn, Adam's happy lesson.

JUDITH

Thou hast learnt sweeter words, not the venom
Which thou didst not so long ago prefer.

QUINEY

And thou hast not thus hit my pate e'en once.

JUDITH

How could we continue in such a bliss?
We would be bored with each other by noon!

QUINEY

If thou wouldst marry me, we could argue
with merry married arguments and pains,
'cept accompanied by a bridal bed
To soften all of our hard diatribes.

JUDITH

And thus we hit upon thy true purpose!

QUINEY

Nay, my purpose is nestled in thy heart.

I do have forkéd tongue, though, I confess,
But perhaps on this holy mountain hot,
We canst place hands on the adder's sweet hole
And we shant hurt, nor shall we e'er destroy.

JUDITH

Art thou even marrying sort, sweet Tom?

QUINEY

Why, yes, my name doth e'en confess it all.
Thomas means twin, so since thou hast lost thine,
I'm thy new pair, thus now to me align.

Quiney and Judith kiss.

JUDITH

I—I will return.

QUINEY Dost thou leave so soon?

JUDITH

I am dressed as a man!

QUINEY Then so be it!

JUDITH

Fear not, my newest, freshest love of all,
Thou shalt have a woman's charms, e'en if sharp,
'Though it shall be thee that shalt make me bleed
On our most happy and holy night.
(Judith and Quiney kiss again.)
I did not fathom I could be happy!

Exit Judith.

QUINEY

Even a demon can catch heaven's breeze!
(Enter Hamnet.)
What is it, boy? A message for me?
(Quiney reads the message.)
Tell Margaret Wheeler that I care not for her bastard

child. I am certain it hails not from me. She hath proved a strumpet and deserves her fate. Let her thus labor alone, she will not rob me of the happiness that has now come to fruition!

Exeunt.

Zel Bromley as Jusith Shakespeare and Samuel Schofield as Thomas Quiney. Photo by Brian Randall.

Zel Bromley as Judith Shakespeare and Sam Schofield as Thomas Quiney. Photo by Brian Randall.

Belinda Purdum as Susanna Shakespeare and Shawnda Ludlow Moss as Anne Shakespeare. Photo by Brian Randall.

William Stewart as Hamnet Shakespeare. Photo by Brian Randall.

*

~ V.1 *Inside New Place. Enter Susannah and John.*

SUSANNA

Mother, he comes!

Enter Anne.

ANNE He is too early now!

I did not expect him for three days yet!

Enter Judith.

JJUDITH

Must bedlam break every time he comes?

Many times hast thou seen his ruddy face.

ANNE

The house is not prepared for him yet to come!

JUDITH

Why care? Thy life wast better in the woods.

Why didst thou give up life of Robin Hood's?

ANNE

I did not rob a solitary soul!

JOHN

Or so hast thou us told. Silent art thou

So thou needs not share thy bright treasure gold!

ANNE

Thou art indeed a strange one, Johnny Hall.

JOHN

I'm not the odd one that dressed 'gainst my sex.

JUDITH

There be no great wrong in thus dressing so,

A man's garments are more comfortable.

SUSANNA

And how wouldst thou know that?

JUDITH

Ah, or so would I think, or imagine.

JOHN

Perhaps she goes about with codpiece, too!

JUDITH

Ha, ha, what jest.

SUSANNA Where is thy dear Thomas?

JUDITH

He said that he shall be thus shortly here.

ANNE

For one, I'm happy for thy marriage nigh,
As it hath brought my husband early here.

JUDITH

I wouldst think it 'cause of my happiness.

ANNE

That, too!

JUDITH Thou art less than convincing, no?

ANNE

Then let my truest verdure expressed be:
My little girl thou wast often alone.
Soon after Hamnet's sickness and his death,
Wast thou defiant, wouldst not learn to read
Nor wouldst thou even learn to write thy name.
Thou regressed, didst then withdraw from us all,
Couldst not but touch thee, for then thou wouldst shrink.
It broke my tender heart to see thee thus,
And Will was gone, could not count on his aid.
With thy so changéd nature, timorous,
Till lately I have worried so for thee,

But now I see how joyful thou canst be,
I thank this man, this Thomas Quiney, sir,
And bless the pen that authored this great glee.

JUDITH

I have so oft thought on poor sorrows mine,
That I forget the griefs that plague thee, too.

ANNE

Those times of slings and arrows are not now,
We're fortified against all those past wrongs.
Thou shalt inherit thy dowry of joy.

JUDITH

A dowry bestowed by a mother's hand.

Enter William.

WILLIAM

My Judith, child, hath turned into a bride!

JUDITH

What, address me thus first and not Susann?

SUSANNA

I had my day already, today is thine!

WILLIAM

'Tis so, but do you think I fav'rites play?

JUDITH

Hath that not been the study of our life?

WILLIAM

Nay, I but love thee each in my own way,
Differently, not to be so compared.

JUDITH

I will tell thee when Thomas arrives here.

Exit Judith.

SUSANNA

We will speak with her words that will aright.

ANNE

Speak gently, betrothéds are tender so.

Exit Susanna and John.

WILLIAM

Thus, we are alone, wouldst thou have it so?

ANNE

When thou didst last go, I said terr'ble words
That I regret and wish I could erase.

WILLIAM

Then thou art not still thus angry with me?

ANNE

Thou didst once speak of a small, fragile bird,
That fled in flight from giant's finger strong,
He meant no wrong, though. Who is the small bird,
'Tis you or I? I know not which it is,
Nor do I know the lumb'ring giant, kind.
We both have played the victim and fright.
Yet I thought of thy tale the other day
When I heard a crash 'gainst our window hard,
And looked outside to spy a humming bird
In pain under our pane, so crumpled, hurt.
A magic bird, not native to our land,
It must have been brought here on merchant's ship
And escaped to only find tragedy.
Put it to death, out of its misery,
Was my first aching, sad inclination,
But I stayed my most rash and killing hand.
I pitied it and couldst not execute,
So I then scooped it up, and gently cupped,
While singing songs it was too weak to join.
I felt in my heart, pray a miracle.

I placed my hand upon its body soft,
As if it had an issue of bad blood
That just needed my healing touch to cure.
To my amazement, as I walked it 'bout,
A strength came again to its tiny frame,
And it did fly from my protecting hand
Much faster than I've ever seen birds fly,
So far, so fast that no more could I see
What distant Elysium it did find.
Are miracles not always parting seas,
But sometimes small, beautiful purities?

WILLIAM

What lesson am I to take from this joy?

ANNE

That betimes, even after it is hurt,
The bird can still thus fly.

WILLIAM

Aye, to thy lips!

(William and Anne kiss.)

I've gifts for thee, some olive branches pure
Unneeded now.

ANNE What couldst thou have for me?

WILLIAM

The only poor gift that comes from poor heart,
Poor shadows compared to thy richest light.

William hands Anne several manuscripts.

ANNE

Plays?

WILLIAM Unlike those I have thus writ before.

There is a new style, tragi-comedy,
That dwells not on death, nor on raucous mirth,

But seeks an honest, gentle, blended tale,
And yet full of magic and wonder still.

ANNE

What hath these players' tales to do with me?

WILLIAM

I've writ these plays for thee, dear Anne.
In these black lines with winsome shadow thine
I played, and then did create these new plays.
All's Well End's Well, Cymbeline, Winter's Tale,
As well as part of this play *Pericles,*
These plays are thine, champion virtue thine,
Which oft wast accuséd by jealousy.
In them thy copy stands tall 'gainst my faults.
My pitch revealed against thy brightest sun.
These, children mine, I birthed with shadow thine,
And thus belong in thy custody true.
I deed them to thy most sage judgment true.
Thou shalt have seat of utmost honor high,
When thou shalt spy thy heirs on platformed Globe.
They are my gift, ever to thee, my love,
My lasting tribute when mortal'ty's gone.
When both of us are cradled in the grave,
These shadows shall appear and our love save

Enter Judith, Quiney, Susanna, and John.

JUDITH

"Papa," come meet the man I leave thee for,
As thou didst leave us.

SUSANNA

Judith, sour not this joy with conflict harsh.

JUDITH

He I shall cleave unto, nevertheless.

WILLIAM

And then be one. But we have met before.

ANNE

Thou hast?

WILLIAM

In bitterness, but now that's past.

Come near me, Thomas, we're now family.

QUINEY

Good morrow, Master Shakespeare, unto thee.

WILLIAM

Good morrow.

QUINEY How fare thee?

WILLIAM Passing well, gramercy.

QUINEY:

Good speech! Are we done?

WILLIAM Aye, I am satisfied!

ANNE:

To deeper matters get to!

WILLIAM I suppose.

I now think on thy father. Good man, he.

QUINEY

There aren't good men, but he was fair enough.

WILLIAM

None good?

QUINEY If New Testament be believed.

I do admit, I am a skeptic there.

WILLIAM

This is the man will marry our Judith?

ANNE

Be patient, Will.

QUINEY

Be not patient, slow Will!
Care not what thou dost think of my true suit.
I have already won the maid I want,
I need not woo thy heart in addition.

WILLIAM

True spoken like a head strong Lysander.
I would not seek to bar determined love.

QUINEY

Then there is no dispute.

WILLIAM

I confess so,
Though, I do not like strutting pride like this.

QUINEY

Pride? I need not an audience, like thee.

SUSANNA

O Judith, wilst thou restrain such anger?

JUDITH

And why, when he doth speak the honest truth?

QUINEY

Thou seest, meddling, matronhead, so marked,
That Judith be not of thy weaker mind,
But is strong in hypocrisy's base face.

SUSANNA

Dost thou accuse me of hypocrisy?

QUINEY

Aye, thou doth take after a hypocrite,
Much in the image of thy father fool!
He, flap mouthed, fobbing fable making ape
That enchants gullible, dull masses, dupes!
A wizard's lies, presenting peeping stone,
Thus, telling King Mob fancies that he scries therein.

False prophet, pretender, base charlatan!

SUSANNA

Canst thou thus listen how he dishonors
Our dear Papa, e'en within his hearing?

JUDITH

He reaps dishonor who sows dishonor.

SUSANNA

And she who betrays won't such mercy get!
A Regan, Goneril, thou art indeed,
'Though we once resisted thus naming thee.

QUINEY

Thou ign'rant, babbling-mouthéd, flap-dragon,
I extinguish thy burning, fury hot
With single swallow, lick of my sweet lips!
Thy flighty flourishes are thus seen
For womanish wails that they truly be!

JOHN

Thy filthy, spewing mouth should now be sewn!

QUINEY

O finally! Stone Puritans can speak!

JOHN

Thou scolds this stone silence of mine, 'tis true,
I cannot speak when thou dost prattle on.
I cannot breathe, thou hast sucked up the air!

ANNE

Whence comes this new, rude behavior, Thomas?
Thou wast willing to play the gentleman
When thou didst come to our New Place before,
But now thou hast a new mouth, a new face
I recognize not when set with before.

QUINEY

It is that man, his foxship, rogueship, him,
That sparks this fury now within my heart!
Before thou wert but baubles, poppets tame,
But then I saw the spoilt, mad, screaming child
That possesses thee, and now I do rage
At the mild way thou dost take his abuse.

ANNE

Abuse? It's thou that art now red in face!
He hath not said a word 'gainst thy nothings,
All fury, sound, by an idiot told!

WILLIAM

Judith?

JUDITH Do not think thou hast my defense.

SUSANNA

Dissembling Brutus. Judas-Judith, she!

WILLIAM

My daughter.

SUSANNA Sister no more.

WILLIAM Sister still.

JUDITH

Thou speakest well, thou hast always spoke well,
But when it mattered, presence needed then,
But not attended.

WILLIAM My faults are plain, true.

Canst forgive them?

JUDITH Canst black be made to white?

WILLIAM

My hands are stained with ink. Wilt forgive me?

JUDITH

A braying ass, though speaks, is yet an ass.

WILLIAM

I am an ass. But wilst thou forgive me?

QUINEY

She will thus not!

WILLIAM I've not ill-used thee, sir!

I was just willing to adopt thy name
Into our home, crest, and dear family.
I was to treat thee tenderly, with care,
For thou didst win my daughter's love, good sworn.

QUINEY

A love I cherish beyond all my goods,
'Though it be attached to a name I hate.

WILLIAM

Why hate? Why must I still be hated thus?
Why is my once good name the scorn of fools?
Am I a crow, truly, grief's harbinger?
Jealousy, disapproval, rivalry,
I'm tired of all such contention, grieved!
I desire to be of gentle peace.
Wilt thou make peace with me, Thomas Quiney?

QUINEY

Dost play the victim? Fortune's poor, poor fool?
The man that lives in such a big, bold house,
The second largest frame in Stratford's shire?

ANNE

He bought it broken down then, by my troth,
A discount deal, I did make sure of that.
'Tis my hard work that made its splendor now.

QUINEY

The man that doth save needed malt in barns
Whilst, desperate, his neighbors hunger thus!

ANNE

That, too, the doing of my cunning hand.
Dost thou think Will is good at numbers? Ha!
I wrest with bus'ness in this family,
So forgive a mother ensuring her
dear Fam'ly's future e'en o'er neighbors poor.
Will signed his name, that is all. I, the rest.

JUDITH

The man that left his struggling fam'ly here,
His son, in his errant absence, did die!

ANNE

I told him to: leave, save this family!

WILLIAM

Nay, I must answer that one for myself,
'Though stirs me to hear love and loyalty
From my fair friend, my best and only wife.

ANNE

I'll roar in the midst of thy enemies.

WILLIAM

And I will kiss that roaring mouth.

William and Anne kiss.

JUDITH

Where was this kiss for Hamnet's dying gasps?

WILLIAM

True, I was away from my dear, sweet Prince,
When angels took his broken form to Heav'n
To be healéd. 'Tis true, I can't deny.
Delayed by plague, messenger could not find
My troupe as we traveled through England's towns
And I received the word too late, too late,
Everlastingly late, my lasting shame.

Thou canst devise no punishment more keen
Than anguish that I felt in that moment
I discovered that I thus failed my son.
If thou dost think me worthy of more pain,
Here is my back, to thy sharp whip thus lain.

A knock is heard.

QUINEY Fail not, Judith. His words are as sweet as ever, but they are poison. How many maidens hath he thoughtlessly killed with those words upon a stage? He will thus murder thy heart!

JUDITH I know no—He is my fathe—

Another knock.

WILLIAM Aye, thy loving father.

QUINEY Who will disappoint you but again! And again! And again!

JOHN

And this man shall be a sure foundation?

QUINEY Thou statue, no one hath asked thee to come to life!

JOHN

If I am yet a statue, I shall be
a rock of offense and thus fall on thee!
I shall grind thee to powder and to dust!

Another knock.

SUSANNA

Do noxious knockers know when they're ignored?

Exit Susanna.

ANNE

Judith, please, if thou dost so marry him,
Do not give way to him demanding thee
To sacrifice us as the dowry dark...

JUDITH Nay, thou wast not the sacrifice. Hamnet was the sacrifice, the lamb, the Isaac beneath that man's cruel blade! I will not forget him, I cannot forget him!

WILLIAM Judith!

JUDITH Do not follow me!

Exit Judith.

QUINEY And now thy good part is mine, great Shakespeare. With thy heart pluck'ed from thy rotting chest, I shall leave the dowry of all the rest.

Exit Quiney. Enter Susanna.

SUSANNA

A dire message for thee, Father, it was.
The Theatre, the Globe, it hath been burnt.
The world thou didst create hath been baptized,
Not with Noah's scouring, destructive flood,
But Apocalypse's fast, purging fire,
Down to its once thought secure foundations.
I am sorry to be a herald dark,
Now forced to confess such a blazing torch.

There is silence, until:

WILLIAM

Care not I. I must go attend Judith.

Exeunt.

*

~ V.2 A pantomime of Judith's marriage. All are in attendamce, including Hamnet.

*

~ V.3 *Inside New Place. Enter William and John.*

WILLIAM

Little Lizzie is like a lizard lithe,
Once caught in hand, she escapes thy grasp still!

JOHN

Aye, and her energy never abates.

WILLIAM

A sweeter, smiling child I never saw.

JOHN

As her grandfather, thou art prejudiced,
But as her father, I must thus agree.

WILLIAM

'Tis good to have thee as our son-in-law,
to balance out the other baggage base.

JOHN

But do not let Thomas hear you say such,
He is but in the other room.

WILLIAM I know.

But when hast he cared about what he says
'Bout me, whether I can hear him or no?

JOHN

Best to make peace, the marriage is now done.

WILLIAM

'Tis what my brain says, but heart rages still.
Of hopes with my Judith, he wrecked the ship.
I thought to repair all with daughter mine,
But even like today when she comes o'er,
Yet her eyes never meet me, nor her mouth
Dare deign to speak with me anytime hence.
The day I gave her to that wretched man

I have never seen her smile upon me,
E'en for the smallest, quietest moment.

JOHN

'Tis a hard nut to crack. Speak something else.
Thou spoke of shipwrecks, I read of just such
A barque thus lost at sea, then happ'ly saved!
A strange isle spoken of, I saved the sheet
Here in my sack, as I thought to give thee.
Perhaps there is a play wreckaged therein.

WILLIAM

I thank ye. They were saved, you thus do say?

JOHN

Every soul. So then lose not your hope,
If Providence can save those sailors lost
Perhaps it can still smile on daughter thine
And repair all you think you have thus lost.

WILLIAM

Think ye so?

JOHN It can do no harm to hope.

WILLIAM

O hope can harm when we give it such sway,
Its winds oft send us dangerous, wild way

There is yelling within.

JOHN What din is this?

Enter Anne.

ANNE

There has been a dread message sent to us.
Margaret Wheeler and her unborn child
Are dead.

WILLIAM

Poor souls, that is a tragedy.

But why screams within? She was naught to us.

ANNE

She was something to Thomas, it is said.

WILLIAM

What? The rogue had a child, but told us not?

Enter Susanna.

SUSANNA

She'll kill him in her mad fury, I fear,
If we do nothing to thus abate it!
In thy room I put Lizzie, don't protest,
I don't want her to witness murder's blood!

Enter Quiney, chased by Judith.

JUDITH

Thou piggish, pusillanimous puttock!
Didst keep her scarlet bed warm all the while
Thou circled my crippled, carrion heart?
Thou impure unction, thou base hypocrite!
Thou didst act so full, high, and heroic!
While thou wast tearing others' towers down,
Thy turrets were tottering off themselves!

QUINEY

Away from me, thou fitchew, clapper-claw!
I know thy hand, I'll not suffer it more!

JUDITH

Then thou shalt know my foot, elbows, and teeth!
They shall be thy new bosom companions!

QUINEY: I plead thee, Master Shakespeare, assist me!
I know thou art a man of peace and love,
What wrongs e'er I did, I deserve not this!

WILLIAM

Dost thou ask of me my good mercy now?

A woman's dead, and her child stillborn, too,
Both deserved father's, husband's protection,
But instead thou didst cast them idly off,
And left them to inherit grief and death!
Thou didst add more wood to those licking flames
And brought my daughter to live in thy swamps,
Which makes her unwitting accessory
To thy most heinous, hideous, hard hate!
My daughter's honor hath been abused thus;
A poor, destitute mother murdered was
By thy neglect and indifference base;
A poor, sweet cherub did not see its sire
Before its eyes fluttered in shade of death,
And thou dost dare beg for our forgiveness?

ANNE

As thou didst, William.

WILLIAM

Nay, nay, not so!
Do not compare my crimes to scarlet his!
After I discovered thou wast with child,
Did I so treat thee? Did I refuse thee
And leave our girl to raise thyself, alone?

ANNE

Thou didst take convincing, and there were times
When I did truly raise these cubs myself.

WILLIAM

Is this how I am remembered, am thanked?

ANNE

When we are instructed to forgiveness,
Dost thou then stoop down and pick up a stone?

WILLIAM

Yet thou obviously forgives not me!

ANNE

Nay, not true, I love thee with all my heart...

WILLIAM

And then thou dost wrack me again with guilt!

JUDITH

Now, both ye, stop it! Thomas, go thy way.

QUINEY

I am thy husband—

JUDITH

Aye, my husband dear,

Which is why I'll not scratch nor mar thee more.

QUINEY

Please, Judith, thou dost know I adore thee.

JUDITH

I know it, aye. I have seen it burn true.
Perhaps we can reconstruct—but not now.
The dust still doth fly o'er the riven oak,
And I cannot see clearly with these eyes,
Now full of motes, sharp slivers, and sharp tears.
Both being blind, we must avoid the ditch.

QUINEY

I am no devil! Nay, cast me not out!

JUDITH

Nay, neither angel, but some creature wet.

QUINEY

Even my friend the moon hath turned away,
But greatest pain is thy betrayal base.

JUDITH

Thus feeling betrayed, thou dost now forget

It was thy secret blade that cut me first.

QUINEY

I'll wait for thee on my lost isle alone,
And hope to see thy sails against the sun.

JUDITH

And whether thou shalt forever thus wait,
Or receive unreserved forgiveness, I…
… know not yet. Higher courts than my poor wits
Shall try this case of thy outcast, lost soul,
And whether it shall remain in exile.

Exit Quiney.

WILLIAM

Bring not such monsters back into thy life!

JUDITH

'Tis my sad choice to make, not subject thee.

WILLIAM

I wish I had such power, control then,
That I could protect thee always from him!
If I had magics, bright divinations,
He would receive such cramps, sharp pains from me!

ANNE

Take care, Will, such dark vengeance can't be ours...

WILLIAM

She is our daughter, our flesh, our own blood,
If we cannot avenge her now, when so?
That skainsmate to rogues!

SUSANNA

Be careful, thou grow scarlet, Papa, red...

JUDITH

I need not thy mangled protection, nor thy vanity's

fury flung at him!

WILLIAM

Dost thou not understand, dearest Judith?

I failed Hamnet, I will not so fail thee!

Agh! *William collapses.*

JUDITH Father?

SUSANNA Papa!

ANNE Will!

They rush to William.

*

~ V.4 *Inside New Place. William is at a desk, writing. Anne enters with soup for William.*

ANNE William...

William lifts a finger. AWilliam finishes and takes the soup.

WILLIAM I thank ye.

ANNE Intent, thou art.

WILLIAM

I desire to do this one good and right.

ANNE

But remember what the doctors told thee.

Thy writing could well make thee feverish.

WILLIAM

It would be more anxiety not to.

When shadows jig so fast in my old pate,

I must give them place for their merriment;

But their music's thrummings are now cut off;

I believe this Galliard is now done.

A play I've finished, as it finished me.

ANNE

Thou art speaking strange...

WILLIAM

Fear not, I am well.
Now that I am finished with this bus'ness,
There is yet more to attend to tonight.
Wouldst thou call our dear girls and John in here?

ANNE

What foreboding is cold upon thy brow?

WILLIAM

I am to shed my belongings and craft
Before I shed my skin.

ANNE

Riddles… help me!

WILLIAM

Call them in then I shall make it all plain.
(Exit Anne.)
Death's song doth not haunt me, but enchants so.
I'm not afraid, I have peace in my God.
How e'er other men see my words and acts,
I know that God hath bright, forgiving eyes
That wink at faults when men's clean hearts be true.
How close comes the refreshing, cooling shade
That shall release me as my light doth fade.
(Enter Anne, Judith, Susanna, and John.)
Here, Lear-like, I do slowly crawl to death...

SUSANNA

Nay, father, thou hast not Lear's old, grey head,
But thou hast many decades in thy heart...

WILLIAM

A celebration if so, jubilee!
Yet I have felt the words drain out of me,
My pen can no longer thus ramble on,
The blood of my sentences dry, is gone.

ANNE

What business to finish didst thou wish?

WILLIAM

A will from Will hath been drawn up today,
And I desired to thus tell thee of it,
That there are no surprises to be had.
My Judith, I once drew thee evenly
To match thy sister's bulk of fortune mine,
But now I tell thee plain: I trust him not.

JUDITH

I know, this I sore expected from thee.

WILLIAM

Be not bitter, please, I have provided
For thee a way to be upheld in life.
Since thou expressed reconciliation,
And he will never be acceptable
To honest, scrutinizing vision, mine,
I can't trust Thomas to not waste all this
That's meant to sustain my fam'ly, my dears.
I have given thee funds denied thy Tom;
Its interest provide thee money long,
And comfort for the rest of thy sweet days.
The house I gave dowry to him and thee
Can also be exchanged for currency,
If thou shouldst ever want to give it up.
Sly Thomas has cruel hampered us in this,
But let it be clear, thou art pure to me

And guiltless of the wrongs done to thy heart.
John?

JOHN Aye, sir.

WILLIAM

Where Thomas hath now proved vile,
Thou hast proven trustworthy and pure gold.
As thou hast taken Susannah to thee,
I plead help my whole family anon.
Thou art thus legal executor now,
Dependent upon Puritan virtue.
To Susanna, 'Lizabeth, and thee goes
the rest of the estate.

SUSANNA What of mother?

WILLIAM

The law gives her a third of the estate,
And she hath properties deeded to her
In a previously wrought arrangement,
But I give her one last thing in the will.

ANNE

What's that?

WILLIAM

I give her the second-best bed.

JUDITH

That's all, and then only the second best?
Dost thou so slight the mother of thy seed?

ANNE

Nay, contrary, he hath not slighted me,
That was our most sweet, well-loved wedding bed.

JOHN

And a most valuable piece at that!

SUSANNA

Dost thou often appraise furniture thus?

JOHN

So, I like comfortable furnishings.

WILLIAM

Comfort did I receive in it.

ANNE So I.

SUSANNA

Again, this kind of talk is not for us!

WILLIAM

Pardon, but I pray all thee to thus know
The Muse thy mother's love hath been to me,
How often her shadow was on my stage
And in my sonnets. There hath been no truth
When her virtue and worth hath been in doubt.
Her statue is erected in my heart,
And there stone hath turned into flesh and blood.
The shadow and its caster are the same,
One smoothly leading into the other.
She is my Hermione, Juliet, too,
My Ros'lind, Desdemona, Thaisa,
Both Helenas, and Portia, mine, most wise,
My laughing Beatrice, my Imogen,
She's all my love that spilled upon a stage,
She is who gives me hope and calms my rage.

ANNE

I thought thou said thou didst run out of words.

WILLIAM

She hath also been my most true critic.

ANNE

Tonight, my criticism is all gone

Joy is happ'ly had, I will not disturb,
Unless I step in with intruding kiss.

William and Anne kiss.

WILLIAM

One last gift to bestow, a document,
Though not a tedious, contentious will,
But rather one last play, *The Tempest* called.
Thou shalt find a lovely daughter in there,
That reflects how I feel about my own.

JUDITH

And how dost thou truly feel 'bout thy kin,
When thou shalt be gone once the Spring comes in?

WILLIAM

Nay, I will never be thus gone again.

JUDITH

What sayest thou?

WILLIAM

I told my players dear to seek a new
Word Smith that shall breathe in their clay new life;
Though, I will knight heirs, my last words imbue,
Lend my final verbs to their plays of strife.
Thus, I may have shipwrecked on magic isle,
Banished and sep'rated from childhood's land,
There I learned magics, an enchanted style,
But now I see Salvation's ship from sand.
I inward know that I must crack my staff,
And in the sea cast off my drownéd book,
But in return, shall hear my children laugh,
And bask in my belovéd's bonny look.
Thus, though I may have some last whispers, gasps,
Know that play in thy hands is sure my last.

JUDITH

Thou shalt stay in Stratford and be with us?

WILLIAM

For as long as I can stay in this skin.

Judith embraces William, weeping.

JUDITH

That is all I ever wanted from thee.

SUSANNA

Soft, list of the characters' list herein...
There is only one daughter in this tale.
Which one of us is she?

JUDITH

Wilt leave it be?

WILLIAM

Fear not, daughters, I have writ thee in one,
Thus weaving in both of thy journeys hard.
As one I love thee and as one devote
Thy images on the shrine of my heart.

SUSANNA

I am yet the favorite.

JUDITH Nay, not so!

Thou hast been dethroned!

WILLIAM

Peace! Let us have peace!

Exit Judith and Susanna, bickering.

JOHN

They inherited, William, thy gift:
Thy fam'ly can multiply many words.

Exit John.

ANNE

And thus tale fulfilled, all's well that ends well.

Husband, wilt thou come to bed?

WILLIAM: Aye, to bed.

(Exit Anne.)

And when I am fin'ly still 'neath that sheet
Which shall wind me and wrap, o'er cover me,
Then shall I know if I but dreamt this strife.
Shall I waken anew, breathe with fresh life
Upon a young Globe that shall appear there?
O will this Will new feet walk, new eyes see?
To bed, to bed! Will I fin'ly find there
The love I sought, waiting for her, from her?
Art thou, bed, perfection, pure affection,
Or wilt thou give me cold slumber, a sleep
That is second-best, second-rate, dreamless, and dark?
Or will I be harrowed with guilt and fire?
For I wrapped tiger's heart in dark desire
And in faithless, cruelest inconstancy
I broke my rhyme into scattered pieces, which did remove and drive away my own wife and children. Perhaps we are all crows, hastening to overdress our black. Thus can it be that my father and mother were mistaken in their faith and deceived by preying ministers who clamored for tithes, indulgences, and absolution? Was the Universal story they didst tell me a child's fable, believed only by those desperate and benighted with grief and fear? Or were humble prayers and rosaries acknowledged, counted to their benefit by a Providence proved true? Or still yet did Queen Bess speak aright when she did shrive her father's adulteries and lift this once chained isle into

bloody right, cutting us from the bands of broken bishops and lost apostles? Was her father's Protest pureborn? Or did it bear the mark of his iniquitous Original Sin? Or...?

Or is there purpose to this forcéd form
That holds my heart in place, in battered hope?
To bed, to bed, will I find love therein,
Her soft arms, all along, to enclose me?
Now as I sought, desp'rate, that prayer from thee,
I Prosp'ro, Ros'lind, Puck, all sent to gain
From thy wrapped hands, hearty approbation,
I still stand in tense anticipation,
And place hot coal on tongue that shall purge sin,
Drive out spirits that now my heart, herein,
Live like cock-sure Legion upon a stage
Who now blacken thy eyes, bleed from the page.
Or, are these not demons but holy dreams,
These visions like emblems, partakest thou
In thine own bed, in thine own restless sleep?
We, mutual waking, break the wall built
'tween you and I, that kept our sep'rate worlds.
That veil ripped now, view my carnates and me,
My Mind's Spirits, poured out of the temple
That contained us in our imagined spheres.
Let us step up to thee in plain, bright view.
My eyes meet with no shame, see my spirit,
And ponder us which seemed but phantom forms.
Now since thou doth witness me, and I thee,
We tell each other what we truly be.

Finis.

Bradley Moss as William Shakespeare.
Photo by Emily Drew.

Shawnda Ludlow Moss as Anne Shakespeare.
Photo by Brian Randall.

Bradley Moss as William Shakespeare
and Hyrum Stewart as Hamnet Shakespeare.
Photo by Brian Randall.

Bradley Moss as William Shakespeare and Shawnda Moss as Anne Shakespeare. Photo by Emily Drew.

Shawnda Moss as Anne Shakespeare,
Peter F. Christensen as John Hall,
and Belinda Purdum as Susanna Shakespeare.
Photo by Brian Randall.

Sam Schofield as Thomas Quiney
and Zel Bromley as Judith Shakespeare.
Photo by Brian Randall.

Sam Schofield as Thomas Quiney.
Photo by Emily Drew.

Bradley Moss as William Shakespeare.
Photo by Brian Randall.

Sam Schofield as Thomas Quiney.
Photo by Brian Randall.

Zel Bromley as Judith Shakespeare.
Photo by Emily Drew.

Zel Bromley as Judith Shakespeare.
Photo by Brian Randall.

Belinda Purdum as Susannah Shakespeare
and Peter F. Christensen as John Hall.
Photo by Brian Randall.

*Shawnda Ludlow Moss as Anne Shakespeare.
Photo by Emily Drew.*

Zel Bromley as Judith Shakespeare, Peter Christensen as John Hall, Belinda Purdum as Susanna Shakespeare, Bradley Moss as William Shakespeare amd Shawnda Moss as Anne Shakespeare. Photo by Brian Randall.

Zel Bromley as Judith Shakespeare and Sam Schofield as Thomas Quiney. Photo by Brian Randall.

Belinda Purdum as Susanna Shakespeare.
Photo by Emily Drew.

Zel Bromley as Judith Shakespeare and Sam Schofield as Thomas Quiney. Photo by Brian Randall.

Foreground: Sam Schofield as Thomas Quiney and Bradley Moss as William Shakespeare. Background: Zel Bromley as Judith Shakespeare and Shawnda Moss as Anne Shakespeare. Photo by Brian Randall.

Belinda Purdum as Susanna Shakespeare and Shawnda Moss as Anne Shakespeare. Photo by Emily Drew.

Zel Bromley as Judith Shakespeare and Sam Schofield as Thomas Quiney. Photo by Brian Randall.

Belinda Purdum as Susanna Shakespeare, Peter F. Christensen as John Hall, Shawnda Moss as Anne Shakespeare, and Bradley Moss as William Shakespeare. Photo by Brian Randall.

William Stewart as Hamnet Shakespeare.
Photo by Emily Drew.

Bradley Moss as William Shakespeare.
Photo by Brian Randall.

Zel Bromley as Judith Shakespeare,
Bradley Moss as William Shakespeare,
Belinda Purdum as Susanna Shakespeare,
Shawnda Moss as Anne Shakespeare,
and Peter F. Christensen as John Hall.
Photo by Brian Randall.

AFTERWORD

"My Year of Shakespeare"

by Mahonri Stewart

INTRODUCTION

As a student, an educator, a playwright, and a human being, William Shakespeare's life and work has held particular significance for me. I have been watching, reading, and studying his plays in earnest since I was 14. Ever since my middle school drama teacher Albert Ricci—as well as my theater and literature loving sister Sarah—lit my initial candle of desire to truly understand Shakespeare, I have reveled in his vaulting use of language; his intimate understanding of human nature and psychology; his uncanny way of constructing a story; and his complex, vulnerable, and often hilarious characters.

Shakespeare centers his plays on the human: on our outer relationships, on our most inward thoughts, on our search for meaning in a seemingly meaningless world. Whether it's Benedict and Beatrice's playfully verbal volleys; Imogen's horror at a beheaded corpse she mistakes for a loved one; Lear's discovery of wisdom through madness; Marina's valiant, virtuous stands against her would-be rapists; Richard II's pitiful, yet oddly soulful journey to self-destruction; Macbeth's back sliding, hardening heart; Hamlet's desperate grief and introspection; or Viola's yearning for her lost brother; I have been caught up in Shakespeare's strangely spiritual-Humanist characters and their struggles, not unlike how Prospero and Miranda were caught up in a tempest and deposited on an enchanted isle of such bewildering and bewitching characters. Shakespeare makes me feel like a shipwrecked wanderer in a land that is equally ferocious and beautiful.

During the year from 2015-2016, particularly, I made a concentrated effort to immerse myself in Shakespeare's work (serendipitously during the same year as the 400th anniversary of his death). I made sure to read, listen to, and/or view his entire canon of plays and sonnets. Most of them I had experienced several times already, in one form or another, but there were a number that were new. *King John, Two Noble Kinsmen, Troilus and Cressida, Timon of Athens,* etc. are plays that, rightly or wrongly, do not receive the same kind of attention as Shakespeare's playlist of greatest hits. Yet, even in the minor plays, there is great sophistication and power in Shakespeare's writing that ought to make any self-aware author envious. Some of these neglected plays—*Measure for Measure* and *Richard II,* for example—I count as masterpieces that rival even his most famous and celebrated plays in their proficient skill and insight.

During this time, I also manically read biography after biography, trying to make sense of the smattering of clues we have about his life, culture, and context. James Shapiro, Germaine Greer, Stephen Greenblatt, Jonathan Bates, Michael Wood, Bill Bryson, Stanley Wells, Harold Bloom, Clair Asquith, and so many other literary scholars and historians have been welcome teachers to help me puzzle out some sort of understanding as to who this mysterious, imperfect, fascinating genius was. Their views and interpretations often conflict, making the enigma even more baffling, but that divergence also freed me to think even more creatively than I often do when writing about historical figures. When representing a real person, I try to be as authentic and accurate as I know how to be. I believe "artistic license" is best used as a seasoning, not as a substitute. Yet such a diversity of viewpoints allowed me to look at the Bard through many different lenses, and then wheel back and discover what my own unique vision and interpretation of his life and work would become.

To the initial chagrin of the students of my English classes in San Diego, I portioned out a whole couple of months to focus on Shakespeare, his plays, his history, and his culture. What some of my students first complained about, they later delighted in. Many of them would come to me personally and tell me that my love of the material was infectious. They discovered for themselves why Shakespeare is still, after more than 400 years, a big deal. Not all of them caught the fire, but many more than I first assumed connected to Shakespeare's insight and skillful storytelling. The sparks of this fiery obsession lit others, and I don't apologize for such reckless, Guy Fawkesian pyromania.

All of this Bardophillic focus culminated in *The Drownéd Book*, which received a staged reading at Utah Valley University on the 400th anniversary of Shakespeare's death, to a wonderfully positive response. Then we had another reading, generously sponsored by the Noorda Regional Theater, while I was their Playwright-in-Residence, once again to surprisingly positive beta testers.

I took the audience's notes and insight I received from those experiences and incorporated them into a new draft which eventually was performed by Zion Theatre Company at the Castle Outdoor Amphitheater during the summer of 2017. This time acting as director, along with my cast (many of whom were already Shakespeare lovers and experts), we devilishly spread that explosive bonfire to an appreciative and, in most cases, informed audience (I can thank, in part, the Tony Award winning Utah Shakespeare Festival for a mass of exceptionally trained Shakespeare lovers residing in the unlikely American Intermountain West). It was a wonderful climax to my own personal year of Shakespeare.

MADE MYSELF MOTLEY TO THE VIEW

I can't truly comment objectively on what the experience really did for others. That will always be a seen "through a glass darkly." Yet the process hit a personal place for me—one that that haunts me even now—and that I certainly can comment on with some surety. I found valuable personal insight into my own life and work by exploring the life and work of a master playwright who died 400 years ago. Yet it wasn't his prestige or retrospective glamor as the world's greatest playwright that enamored me. It's easy to get caught up with all of that side of Bardolotry, certainly; but it was an increasing sense I was receiving that Shakespeare was sharing more intimate details about himself through his characters, poetry, and flights of fancy (that may have not been so fanciful) than I had first assumed.

In Sonnet 110, Shakespeare wrote something that still strikes me:

> Alas 'tis true, I have gone here and there,
> And made myself a motley to the view,
> Gored mine own thoughts, sold cheap what is most dear,
> Made old offenses of affections new.[1]

This brief, but vivid sketch portrays Shakespeare—with the assistance of his fellow "motley," patchwork actors—goring his "own thoughts," selling for cheap "what is most dear." It clearly states that Shakespeare certainly did feel that his plays and poems revealed him in a vulnerable, intimate way, and that he was sometimes uncomfortable with that fact.

There are those who like to divorce Shakespeare's personal life from his writing. For example, James Shapiro likes to lean into Shakespeare's biography by looking at the historical events and documents surrounding him,[2] and strongly disfavors the

---

1 Lines 1-4. I am using the volume *Love Poems and Sonnets of William Shakespeare, Illustrated in Color by Vera Bock* (Garden City: Double Day & Company, 1957) as my reference point for the sonnets in this essay.

2 An approach which has worked well for Shapiro in *1599: A Year in the Life of William Shakespeare, The Year of Lear: Shakespeare in 1606,* and *Contested Will: Who Wrote Shakespeare,* all fascinating treatments of Shakespeare within his context. In no way am I slighting Shapiro in this divergence, as I have a

(by its nature) speculative nature of the fusion of biography and literary analysis: "Modern biographers who nonetheless speculate on such matters, or in the absence of archival evidence read the plays and poems as transparently autobiographical, inevitably end up revealing more about themselves than they do about Shakespeare."[3] In this Shapiro makes a very valid point, which I sometimes have had to check myself on in pursuing the writing of this play. Yet I also believe that "revealing more about" ourselves was rather Shakespeare's point. In opening his mind and soul to us, he is helping us understand ourselves. As I have Shakespeare say in the closing lines of the play, "Now since thou doth witness me, and I thee/ We tell each other what we truly be."

It is also plain to me that Shakespeare himself gave indications, like the one found in Sonnet 110, that he did, indeed, invest his life into his work, and his work into his life, blurring any sort of distinction or definitive answer regarding either. There is significant insight in seeking for Shakespeare in his plays to be found, at least for those who are comfortable with possibilities rather than sureties.

Thus, those who refuse to read at least some level of autobiography into Shakespeare's themes, poetry, and characters, have to contend with this compelling sonnet that confesses that Shakespeare's "own thoughts" and lived experiences find place in his poems and plays, expertly hiding shadows of true events among fictional characters and scenarios. It presents clearly how much Shakespeare put of himself on the stage, and I am

---

tremendous respect for his work, from which I have learned a great deal.

3 *The Year of Lear: Shakespeare in 1606* (New York: Simon and Schuster, 2015), p. 12.

convinced that, in many cases, his plays and sonnets are truly parables about his own life, using the metaphor and obfuscation of poetry to create encoded autobiography. Yet, like parables, with every answer, there are many more questions. They give both insight and they incite. They bestow clarity and mystery. They cast light and shadow.

I know, at least, that this has been my own tendency as a playwright and poet. Even when loose autobiography is hidden in a play of mine, sometimes subconsciously, the process of writing naturally brings buried things to the surface, even private details of my life which I am normally shy about. To confess less than that would divorce a writer from all authenticity and introspection in his work. It may be academically in vogue to separate an author from his work, a playwright from her plays, but I know it would be seemingly impossible for me to do so. A playwright's life and environments are her main resource. Study, observation, and bookwork, as strong as they are on their own, are pulled into the gravity of life experience. Even imagination has to shape its masonry from the blocks and stones of lived life.

In Sonnet 110, Shakespeare does show that he had reticence about completely giving away his privacy, to sell "cheap what is most dear." Through his plays, however, he could scratch that itch of self-revelation. Puck-like, he could reveal himself long enough to weave an impish spell, but then pull back into the shadowed forest before completely exposing his secrets. Perhaps the reason we have never found an autobiography or journal in Shakespeare's hand is because he already wrote them in the form of his creative work. His plays are his diary. His sonnets are his personal letters.

This is the approach I took in writing *The Drownéd Book*. I hold a firm belief that, though veiled, the contours of Shakespeare's own face are behind his plays and poetry. Although, as Germain Greer wrote, all attempts at Shakespearean biography are "houses built of straw," she also goes on to interject, "but there is good straw and rotten straw, and some houses are better built than others."[4]

As a result, much in this vein becomes speculative and subject to interpretation. Yet Shakespeare's work is the closest we get to the man himself, and thus it is the best straw we have available. The scant scattering of wills, contracts, and other historical documents that exist are certainly invaluable in understanding Shakespeare the man, and I used them when available. Shakespeare's final will, particularly, was important in my process of divining the history of his final days and the status of his various family relationships at that point in his life. Yet it was always the plays and poems that felt the most personal, that grafted meat, nerves, and skin onto the skeleton of the official record. And it was, indeed, those family relationships that most caught my attention when I decided to focus on the final years of Shakespeare's life as the beginning of my narrative.

FAIR FRIEND

In Sonnet 104, Shakespeare calls the addressee of the poem his "fair friend."[5] This title of "friend" ("older friend,"[6] "dear friend," etc.) reoccurs throughout the sonnets, as Shakespeare

---

4 *Shakespeare's Wife*, (New York: Harper Perennial, 2007), p. 9

5 Line 1.

6 Sonnet 110, line 11.

devotes his lyrical words again and again to this person, this dear friend, who was more than just an object of lust or romantic obsession, but rather a person for whom he had a strong and sturdy respect, with whom he cultivated a lasting relationship. The word "friend," especially when used so constantly and so affectionately as Shakespeare does in the Sonnets, denotes that this person is more than a mere number in a series of paramours. Rather, it shows a more mature relationship than what we would find with, say, the impulsive Juliet and her Romeo (at least "three winters" and "three summers"[7] are referred to in Sonnet 104, indicating that their relationship has existed for at least three years at this point). This is Romeo and Juliet, if they survived and lived those three years together. Shakespeare is able to boil down his feelings for this person into three words: "Fair, kind, and true, is all my argument,"[8] which places as much, if not more, emphasis on the inner qualities as the outer. This was a person that Shakespeare loved on a deeper level than mere surface attraction.

These "Fair Friend" sonnets were meant to be more than tools of seduction or flattery towards a possible conquest, or a poetic exercise voiced in a fictional persona, but rather monuments to a person who, he often confessed, was greater than the shadow-sonnet itself: "Look in your glass, and there appears a face/That overgoes my blunt invention quite…"[9] It was a relationship which seemed deep and meaningful to the playwright and moved beyond phantoms of fantasy to find flesh against flesh.

7 Lines 3-4.

8 Sonnet 105, line 9.

9 Sonnet 103, lines 6-7.

Some may think the "friend" being addressed in Sonnet 104 is either the mysterious "Dark Lady" addressed in various sonnets, or the "Young Man," who many posit to be the Earl of Southampton,[10] a high-born patron of Shakespeare's and a visible mover and shaker in Queen Elizabeth's court. There are also a number of theories that include Southampton as a paramour to Shakespeare, theories often strenuously debated. Now I am not necessarily averse to the theory of Shakespeare having had a momentary relationship with Southampton, if evidence bore that fact out. Many of Shakespeare's sonnets are certainly written to a young man, and evidence connects Shakespeare to Southampton, as Shakespeare openly sought Southampton's patronage. Yet, like Michael Wood,[11] I believe that, in select instances among the sonnets, the "sweet boy" that he is addressing may have rather been his dear son Hamnet, though Hamnet would certainly not fit many of the more romantic poems in the early sonnets that are addressed to a different male muse. In any case, if Southampton is the subject of many of the sonnets, I believe they may have been commissioned work, written in a scenario that appears to have inspired Shakespeare's comedy *Twelfth Night*.

As various sources have already deduced, Shakespeare seems to be writing on behalf of someone who hired him (most likely William Cecil, the 1st Baron of Burghey) to write poetry to his adopted ward Southampton. In this way, Shakespeare was to woo Southampton on behalf of Cecil's granddaughter (all

---

10 For example, see Stephen Greenblatt's *Will in the World: How Shakespeare Became Shakespeare* (New York: W.W. Norton and Company, 2004), chapter 8. Also, Amanda Mabillard, "Shakespeare, William. Sonnet 104." *Shakespeare Online*, 8 Dec. 2012. < http://www.shakespeare-online.com/sonnets/104detail.html >, accessed August 7, 2015.

11 *In Search of Shakespeare*, (DVD. Directed by Michael Wood. PBS Home Video, 2005).

so Cecil could access even more of Southampton's fortune).[12] I think the most telling clue that *Twelfth Night's* writing-on-behalf-of-another is a mirror to Shakespeare's own status as a wooer comes from the striking similar passages in both *Twelfth Night* and the sonnets. In *Twelfth Night,* we find Viola (dressed as a man, of course) pressured to woo Olivia on behalf of her beloved master Orsino. In trying to pry Olivia away from her hermit-like state, Viola appeals to her vanity, claiming that if Olivia leaves no "copy" (child) of such a beauty, she will be depriving the world of a rich jewel:

> Lady, you are the cruell'st she alive
> If you will lead these graces to the grave
> And leave the world no copy.[13]

Similarly, in the first dozen or so of the sonnets, Shakespeare writes to Southampton, playing to his vanity in a that familiar vein, arguing that if Southampton continues in his stubborn bachelorhood, he will not pass down his image for future generations to admire in his children. This early series within the sonnets culminates to an echo of the image utilized in *Twelfth Night*:

> She carved thee for her seal, and meant thereby
> Thou shouldst print more, not let that copy die.[14]

Thus, we find two very similar scenarios and the imagery of a "copy" linking *Twelfth Night* to the early sonnets, creating what is likely an autobiographical link between the two.

---

12 See Greenblatt's *Will in the World,* chapter 8.

13 Act I, Scene 5, lines 228-231

14 Sonnet 11, lines 13-14

It seems that Shakespeare is drawing from the same well of lived experience in both creative endeavors.

It is difficult to conclude either way whether Shakespeare's feelings for Southampton ever blossomed beyond this awkward poet-for-hire situation—there are those that have made compelling arguments in that vein, but there are also obstacles to that conclusion. Yet the sonnets to the Young Man are to a different person, in a different time, for a different purpose, and are situated earlier in the sequence of sonnets than the "Fair Friend" sonnets which pick up very different themes and a very different muse.

The Fair Friend Sonnets come later in the sequence (although, they may or may not be dated to an earlier point in Shakespeare's life), and have various different clues as to whom these sonnets are directed towards. This muse is a subject whose evidence fits neither the Young Man (again, probably Southampton, but in some cases may be his son Hamnet, especially when referred to as "sweet boy"), nor the Dark Lady of some of the later sonnets. I believe it is very clear from the inner context of these sonnets that Anne Hathaway Shakespeare is the prime candidate for this particular run in the sequence. They include details that would apply only to her.

Evidences of particular importance for this argument, which I have not seen pointed out elsewhere, are the sonnets that indicate a married relationship. For example, late into the sequence Shakespeare is in the midst of a series that seem to suspect, without evidence, the Fair Friend's fidelity. At this point in the series, he identifies a rival lover that he suspects, possibly a close friend of his, but vacillates on whether he believes that his beloved could betray him. In Sonnet 91 he states "Thy love is better than high birth to me,"[15] showing how much he has valued her from the beginning, but throughout this section of the sonnets Shakespeare suffers from a crippling fear that this beloved could cheat on him and he would not know it: "But what's so blessed-fair that fears no blot? /Thou mayst be false, and yet I know it not."[16]

Yet, there is a hope he clings to throughout this period of doubt. He states that: "For term of life thou art assured mine,"[17] and also references a "happy title"[18] as part of this assurance. What is this "term of life" and "happy title" that would cause such an assurance, if not a life-long marriage and the titles of husband and wife?

The connection between this building jealousy in the sonnets and a surprising number of Shakespeare's plays where a woman is falsely accused of infidelity by a jealous husband (*Othello*, *Much Ado About Nothing*, *The Winter's Tale*, *Cymbeline*), only to have the woman's honor restored, is important and not accidental. Thematically, again and again, what we find in the sonnets, we often find in the plays, and both indicate a married couple who had a strong, loving marriage, only to have it driven asunder for a time by the husband's jealousy. In every case within the plays, the jealousy is irrational and unfounded. In cases like *Othello*, the tragic consequences were permanent. Yet, in cases like *The Winter's Tale* and *Much Ado About Nothing*, a redemptive ending is given to their love, in

15 Line 9.

16 Sonnet 92, Lines 13-14.

17 Sonnet 92, line 2.

18 Sonnet 92, line 11.

which the flawed man is forgiven after serving a sanctifying penance. This is the story of William and Anne.

And it's not only William's jealousy that has to be dealt with. Anne seems to have had her own complaints to direct towards Will, which are listed quite clearly in Sonnet 117. William has "scanted" the attention Anne deserves from him, and "Forgot your dearest love to call." He has been frequently with "unknown minds," taking time to spend with University Wits, actors, even strangers, when he should have been spending more time with her. "I have hoisted sail to all winds," traveled to other countries without her, "Which should transport me farthest from your sight." Most importantly, William continues in Sonnet 117 that Anne has a "dear purchased right," "bonds." Back then, a wife's right was "purchased" by dowry. A marriage was the most obvious "bond" a person could create with one's beloved. These are the legal words for marriage, but Shakespeare also endows them with emotional and romantic weight.

Again and again in the sonnets we find these key words connecting the Fair Friend as Shakespeare's wife ("term of life," "assured mine," "happy title," "bond," "dear purchased right"), and the record clearly shows that Shakespeare only had one wife; he only had Anne. These clues are so obvious to me when I read the sonnets, I am rather shocked that I have not seen them talked about before. How can hundreds of thousands, perhaps millions of readers have gone over these sonnets and not drawn out that they do, indeed, belong to Anne? Are we so married to the complicated, interpolating interpretations of the past not to see what should be plain from the outset? That a man may write love poems to his wife.

Back to Sonnet 117. Rather than accusing Anne of being a nagging wife, Shakespeare acknowledges in the sonnet that these are indeed her rights, and that he has indeed wronged her with his neglect. The only defense he has to give is in the last (almost) rhyming couplet:

> Since my appeal says I did strive to prove
> The constancy and virtue of your love.[19]

If Shakespeare is not just trying to escape another scolding and can be taken at his word here, then it appears that these faults of his are ways of proving the constancy of Anne's love, a constancy she seems to have well proved.

Suffice it to say that I have found compelling evidence that particularly points to William and Anne having a strong, loving relationship, just as there is evidence in the sonnets and in the plays (particularly, *Othello*, *Cymbeline*, and *Winter's Tale*), that their relationship hit hard times and the "green eyed monster"[20] of jealousy took over, causing Shakespeare to mistrust Anne and believe she was cheating on him, identifying an imagined, rival lover; then Shakespeare, as a result, had his own infidelities with the Dark Lady; only to have their love redeemed, and Anne's supposed infidelities revealed as false accusations, her good name cleared, as Desdemona, Imogen, and Hermione's were.

This is particularly important considering that much ado has been made of the "second best bed" that Shakespeare gives Anne in his final will, and the shrill efforts by scholars like Stephen Greenblatt to cast shade on Anne and her relationship with

---

19 Lines 13-4

20 *Othello*, Act III, Scene III, line 171.

her husband William. In *Will in the World,* Greenblatt writes paragraph after paragraph, page after page,[21] about why he believes all of the marriages and relationships in Shakespeare's plays are doomed and loveless (with the horrifying exceptions of Claudius/Gertrude, Macbeth/Lady Macbeth, and Anthony/Cleopatra), even though many of Shakespeare's plays end happily with marriage (Greenblatt thinks Shakespeare's being ironic in these cases). He moves forward with his assumption that, "There are few happy marriages in all of literature,"[22] and that Shakespeare, in extension, was living in a "forcéd... hell"[23] of a marriage: "It is difficult *not* to read his works in the context of his decision to live for the most of a long marriage away from his wife."[24]

Thus, it was important for me to instill the complexities behind William and Anne's relationship as I explored the tail end of their relationship in *The Drownéd Book*. I went into the project with an open mind in both directions, knowing some of the unresolved controversies that surrounded their marriage. However, as I came across what I found to be overwhelming evidence in Shakespeare's texts, I knew their relationship needed greater nuance and redeeming qualities than even otherwise expert Shakespearean scholars like Greenblatt were willing to give to it.

Anne has been falsely maligned in death, as she was in life, and I hope that I have succeeded in making her a more complex

21 In Chapter 4, particularly, but he takes up the refrain again at later points in the book as well.

22 *Will in the World*, 43

23 Ibid, 123, quoting *1 Henry VI.*

24 Ibid, 140.

figure in my play, rather than the central object of derision that Greenblatt uses her as in his screed against marriage. I love much of Greenblatt's work, and the majority of his insights into Shakespeare's life, but I take objection to his treatment of Anne, and what seems to me to be an obsessively negative spin regarding Shakespeare's representation of marriage.

Unlike Greenblatt, I find a great deal to love about Shakespeare's romantic pairings. Greenblatt disparages and berates Beatrice and Benedict, Rosalind and Orlando, Romeo and Juliet, and Shakespeare's other power couples. Are they perfect? Certainly not. What relationship is? Yet there is a reason that audiences and readers keep going back to their love stories, and it's not because they're deconstructing the relationships with an eternally cynical view of them. Rather, these relationships feel very real on many levels, and have great love and warmth to counteract their realistically portrayed difficulties. Shakespeare did not tend to polarize his views into camps of extremes on any subject, but instead addressed topics and characters with powerful nuance. As Germaine Greer wrote:

> What should be obvious is that Shakespeare did not think in twentieth-century clichés. We are not dealing here with representations of folk as 'happily married', but as truly married. For Shakespeare marriage was a demanding and difficult way of life—if anything, more demanding and more difficult for wives than for husbands.[25]

In the "Fair Friend" series of sonnets that I posit are addressed to Anne—taking place after the *Twelfth Night*-like

25 *Shakespeare's Wife*, 18.

set that are commissioned for the Young Man, and before the Dark Lady[26] sonnets that seem to indicate an affair Shakespeare may have had after he thought Anne had been untrue to him—Shakespeare is often lovingly reflective of his wife.

A number of the sonnets sweetly acknowledge their age difference (Anne was several years older than her husband), as Shakespeare tells Anne that he doesn't care about the age gap, quieting her insecurities:

> To me, fair friend, you never can be old
> For as you were when first your eye I eyed,
> Such seems your beauty still.[27]

And, despite Greenblatt's assertion that the distance that Shakespeare had to travel from Stratford for his work in London was his way to escape Anne, to gleefully place miles between them, the sonnets indicate otherwise. There are several of the sonnets that talk about Shakespeare having to travel away from his beloved, and the pain it caused him:

> How weary do I journey on the way,
> When what I seek, my weary travels end,
> Doth teach that ease and repose to say,
> 'Thus far the miles are measured from thy friend!'
> The beast that bears me, tired with my woe,
> Plods dully on, to bear that weight in me,
> As if by some instinct the wretch did know
> His rider loved not speed, being made from thee:

26 I certainly believe the Dark Lady theory, that Shakespeare had some paramour for a time. There's ample evidence for this in the sonnets. I believe this happened when he mistakenly thought he had been betrayed by Anne. Yet many of the poems that some attribute to the Dark Lady, I believe actually belong to Anne.

27 Sonnet 104, lines 1-3.

The bloody spur cannot provoke him on
That sometimes anger thrusts in his hide;
Which heavily he answers with a groan,
More sharp to me than spurring to his side;
For that same groan doth put this in my mind;
My grief lies onward, and my joy behind.[28]

Shakespeare shows his grief at parting, portraying it even in his horse's lethargy, and very poignantly expresses that—despite scholarly interpretations that theorize otherwise—Shakespeare was depressed whenever he left his wife. In the next sonnet he contrasts that sadness with the jubilation that came with his return trip:

Thus can my love excuse the slow offence
Of my dull bearer when from thee I speed:
From where thou art why should I haste me thence?
Till I return, of posting is no need.
O, what excuse will my poor beast then find,
When swift extremity can seem but slow?
Then should I spur, though mounted on the wind,
In winged speed no motion shall I know:
Then can no horse with my desire keep pace;
Therefore desire, of perfect'st love being made,
Shall neigh—no dull flesh—in his fiery race;
But love, for love, thus shall excuse my jade;
Since from thee going he went willful-slow,
Towards thee I'll run and give him leave to go.[29]

---

28 Sonnet 50.

29 Sonnet 104, lines 1-3.

And still in the next sonnet, Shakespeare again addresses the time he spends apart from Anne, comparing himself to a man who must spend time apart from his "up-locked treasure"[30] whose lack keeps him in a state of "seldom-pleasure,"[31] their feasts being "so solemn and so rare":[32]

> Since, seldom coming, in the long year set,
> Like stones of worth they thinly placed are,
> Or captain jewels in the carcanet.
> So is the time that keeps you as my chest,
> Or as the wardrobe that which robe doth hide,
> To make some special instant special blest,
> By new unfolding his imprison'd pride.
> Blessed are you, whose worthiness gives scope,
> Being had, to triumph, being lack'd, to hope.[33]

There is an exquisite sense of feeling in these particular sonnets, more personal than the more intellectual, poetic experiments found in Shakespeare's commissioned work for Southampton, as shown in his more famous, but emotionally empty, "Shall I compare thee to a summer's day?" lines in Sonnet 18. Instead of such literary conceits, we find here, in poems like Sonnets 50-52, Shakespeare's lived experience, his feeling of love lost when he and Anne were apart, and then that love won when he returned home again.

The lack, instead of being celebrated, made Anne all the more precious to him. He compares her to "stones of worth,"

30 Sonnet 52, line 2.

31 Ibid, line 4.

32 Ibid, line 5.

33 Ibid, Lines 6-14.

though they are "thinly placed" and rare. Although his life does not allow him to give more place for them because of this rarity, they are yet his "captain jewels." Of equal worth is "the time that keeps you as my chest," which is a lovingly intimate, deeply personal image. Despite the sometimes rocky road of their marriage, most of which Shakespeare later realized he had self-inflicted, William loved Anne, and she loved him.

FAIREST CORDELIA, MOST LOVED, DESPISED

Daughters take up a special place in Shakespeare's plays. On one hand, we have ideals of virtue and wit like Cordelia in *King Lear*, Miranda in *The Tempest*, or Marina in *Pericles*. They are clever and intelligent women, certainly not card board cut outs, nor tabula rasas that can simply be projected upon. Like the vast majority of Shakespeare's characters, they are fascinating individuals that show strength, independence, and capacity. However, they also are raised to a level of heroism and virtue, perhaps slightly absent of the number of tragic flaws that stick to many of Shakespeare's other characters. These capable, but honorable daughters seem dear to Shakespeare's heart and, though human and not without their imperfections, shine a little purer than many of Shakespeare's more colorful brood.

On the other hand, we have daughters like Regan and Goneril in *King Lear*, dark foils to their virtuous sister Cordelia. Yet these two women are not without their complexity as well, and it would be a mistake to cast them melodramatically as sneering, unfeeling villains.

In an insightful essay,[34] Stephen Reid takes a psychoanalytical approach to the sisters and the progression of their behavior. Reid follows what begins as Goneril and Regan's dispassionate, clinical, and *accurate* view of their father King Lear and his faults, with no murderous intent or hatred towards him to begin with, and then follows how the emotional trauma of Lear's rejection of them in their childhood again re-surfaces once they see how even his long-favorite daughter, Cordelia, could also be rejected.

Having been overruled and overlooked all of their lives, and having had to repress the emotional impact of that snubbing for decades, Regan and Goneril now have the power and freedom to be agents unto themselves in a way that was unavailable to them before. Testing their newfound power, and intoxicated by its effects, while also haunted by the insecurities rooted in their father's rages, moods, and unmasked favoritism of their sister Cordelia, Regan and Goneril's chief motivation is to not to be overruled again, which leads to the war of wills between the unstable Lear and his daughters.

It is Lear's tragic flaws as a father that plants these destructive seeds into the body of his family. He is the origin of the web of distress they all find themselves in, and in tragically Shakespearean fashion, it falls heavy upon his head, as well as theirs. Family relationships are often messy, complicated things to begin with, and compound that with the mammoth power and politics behind a royal family, the results in the case of the clan of Lear were devastating.

---

34 "In Defense of Goneril and Regan." *American Imago* 27, no. 3 (1970): 226-44. http://www.jstor.org/stable/26302628, accessed July 31, 2018.

How many of these family dynamics—positive and negative, Cordelia and her sisters—may be reflections of Shakespeare's own family are, of course, out of our reach to definitively state. However, we do get some connective tissue in finding certain patterns that seem to be reflected in his family's life.

Does the fact that Shakespeare's oldest daughter Susanna receives the bulk of the estate in Shakespeare's will cast her as the favored Cordelia of the family? Is Lear's curse, "How sharper than a serpent's tooth it is/To have a thankless child,"[35] a dig towards his younger daughter Judith, all while he praises Susanna?

Or is that matter complicated by the presence of Judith's husband, Thomas Quiney, who Shakespeare went to great lengths to cut out of his will? Does it show that Shakespeare had more disfavor with the man she married, rather than any ill will directed towards his daughter Judith? The fact that Quiney had dishonered Judith by hiding the fact that he had already impregnated a woman, Margaret Wheeler, and then left Wheeler and their child to fend for themselves and then die without his aid; all while courting and then marrying his daughter Judith, would clearly muddy that relationship. Shakespeare made certain that, though he would not trust Quiney with his fortune, Judith and her children would be comfortably set up for the rest of their lives. Does this not show a loving father's care, despite the extremely distressing situation they had all found themselves in?

The matter of the will could have been further complicated with the terms of Susanna's dowry in her marriage to John

35 *King Lear,* Act 1, Scene 4, lines 282-3.

Hall. How much was promised when Shakespeare handed his daughter over to the Puritan doctor? Were Shakespeare's hands bound to a certain degree when it came time to compose his final will?

The distinction between Shakespeare's two daughters reaches back further than Shakespeare's last will and testament, however. One possible, and baffling, difference between the two sisters seems to have been their level of education.

Often anti-Stratfordians—conspiracy theorists who believe that William Shakespeare didn't actually write the works attributed to him, but rather claim that he was a front man for another writer—claim that evidence against Shakespeare's authorship of the plays lies in the claim that his daughters weren't educated. To bolster this claim, they point to a deed of land transfer that Judith's future mother-in-law Bess Quiney called upon her to witness. Judith signs with an X instead of a signature. The anti-Stratfordians point to this as evidence that the daughters of the supposed greatest writer of all time were illiterate. How could this be if Shakespeare truly wrote his works?

There are a couple of problems with this argument. First, Shakespeare was away from his family living in London a great deal, and if there was any lack of education on the part of his girls, it may have been out of economic necessity. As Germain Greer notes:

> Until at least the mid-1590s Shakespeare was certainly not a wealthy man, and no attention would have been paid to providing Judith with an education that she

> did not need. By the time the family acquired New Place, it would have been too late. We may be sure, I think, that Judith could read her Bible, and she evidently couldn't write with a pen, but she might have been able to enter transactions in chalk on a slate or keep track of them with wooden tallies.[36]

In this era, unless public education was available in one's town, as evidence indicates it was for Shakespeare during his childhood, education was for the rich. The Shakespeares did not start out as wealthy, although they would eventually rise to that status through Shakespeare's shares in their acting company, the Lord Chamberlain's Men/The King's Men, and then through other later investements of his money, such as his controversial investement in malt, which was a precious commodity during times of famine that was seen as denying other hungry people in the community. Thus, their family's good fortune was a later development, and educational opportunities were not always spread through their family evenly.

This may be tragic, but at least if Judith could not read, she was not denied the enjoyment of the bulk of her father's work. One did not have to read English to understand Shakespeare's plays, only able to hear and see them. I like the thought of Shakespeare's family occassionally traveling to London to see Will's plays at the Globe, and I wonder if Judith was ever enraptured by what she saw and heard.

Of course, sometimes a prophet is not appreciated in his own country, or among the members of his own household. It's possible if there ever was a rift between Shakespeare and

---

36 *Shakespeare's Wife*, 271.

Judith that she turned away from all that her father was associated with, including reading and writing, and therefore pursued her own interests.

The main problem with the anti-Stratfordian argument about the education of the Shakespeare girls, however, is that although Judith could not write her name, Susanna certainly could. Susanna's signature has survived and is recorded in a strong, beautiful style. To me, this deflates any credibility the argument may have had. Furthermore, Lachlan Mackinnon has found evidence that there was indeed a public school for girls in Stratford during Susanna's time,[37] which bolsters the chance that this signature is a shadow of Susannah's accomplishments there.

Does this show, however, that Susanna once again was the favored child, that she alone received a proper education? Possibly, but there may be an even simpler explanation to all of this, and it has to do with the common trauma and tragedy which the whole family endured: the death of Hamnet.

GOODNIGHT, SWEET PRINCE

Germaine Greer is almost certainly right that "No member of the Shakespeare family would have felt the loss of Hamnet more keenly than his womb-sister."[38] Perhaps Shakespeare is recording the grief he saw his daughter Judith, Hamnet's twin, endure when he so vulnerably expresses Viola's aching loss for the believed death of her twin brother Sebastian. When Duke

37 Paul Edmonton and Stanley Wells, eds., "His Daughter Susanna Hall," *The Shakespeare Circle: An Alternative Biography* (Cambridge: Cambridge University Press), 74-5.

38 "His Daughter Judith and the Quineys," *The Shakespeare Circle*, 110.

Orsino asks Viola/Cesario about her sibling's "history," Viola responds plaintively:

> A blank, my lord...
> I am all the daughters of my father's house
> and all the brothers too...[39]

When Shakespeare describes Viola, it makes one wonder how much of it is a portrait of his inconsolate daughter:

> ...She pined in thought,
> And with a green and yellow melancholy
> She sat like patience on a monument,
> Smiling at grief. Was this not love indeed?[40]

Could have Hamnet's death, the loss of her womb-brother and soul friend, at their vulnerable age of 11 had such a devastating effect on Judith that she withdrew from her studies, lost interest in books and writing, and caused her to abandon other things she may have once found enjoyment in? Perhaps the reason that Judith didn't marry until she was into her thirties was not, as some have suggested, because she was plain,[41] but because she had difficulty maintaining the sort intimacy and trust needed to once again let her heart build a bridge with another person's. This sort of devastated depression is all too common in those who have suffered post-traumatic stress. Its universality, however, makes it no less personal, and no less poignantly painful.

---

39 *Twelfth Night*, Act 2, Scene 4, lines 110, 121-2.

40 Ibid, 112-5.

41 Greer, "His Daughter Judith and the Quineys," *The Shakespeare Circle*, 110.

Perhaps this trauma also caused Judith to withdraw from her family. It may have been a slow drift at first, unperceived by others, but before he knew it, William may have found himself inadvertantly estranged from his daughter. She may have even blamed him for his long absences in London during their storms of grief and long nights of quiet dread. It's likely that he may have not have even been there for Hamnet's death, if it had come suddenly. When his family needed him the most, William may have been acting on a stage for strangers.

Of course, William was suffering his own Purgatory after the loss of his son. In an age when to have an heir that was male still meant something significant, to lose your only son was devastating. Yet that kind of societal pressure was probably only a small part of it. Shakespeare's grief seems much more personal, as evidenced by Constance in *King John* after she, too, loses her young son:

> Thou art not holy to belie me so;
> I am not mad: this hair I tear is mine;
> My name is Constance; I was Geffrey's wife;
> Young Arthur is my son, and he is lost:
> I am not mad: I would to heaven I were!
> For then, 'tis like I should forget myself:
> O, if I could, what grief should I forget!
> Preach some philosophy to make me mad,
> And thou shalt be canonized, cardinal;
> For being not mad but sensible of grief,
> My reasonable part produces reason
> How I may be deliver'd of these woes,
> And teaches me to kill or hang myself:
> If I were mad, I should forget my son,

Or madly think a babe of clouts were he:
I am not mad; too well, too well I feel
The different plague of each calamity.[42]

With Hamnet's death in 1596, and scholars deducing that *King John* was written in the mid-1590s, Constance's dread over her dead son was most likely no coincidence. I believe *King John* followed on the tails of the death of Shakespeare's son, and all the talk of death, madness, and the temptation towards suicide would not end there, but rather torturously percolate for months and years in Shakespeare's brain until William's heart rendings manifested themselves in a work reflective of this great, introspective pain.

Hamlet would premiere in 1599, and its meditations on death, madness, and the resistance against self-slaughter would become legendary. The fact that its protagonist shares the name of Shakespeare's son who died only a few years before, and dwells so much on the relationship between fathers and sons, is perhaps the most damning evidence against the anti-Stratfordians who callously believe that Shakespeare is a fraud, or that his plays have nothing to do with William's personal life and inner world. Hamnet was branded on William's heart, as Hamlet's father was branded on Hamlet's:

...Remember thee!
Ay, thou poor ghost, whiles memory holds a seat
In this distracted globe. Remember thee!
Yea, from the table of my memory
I'll wipe away all trivial fond records,
All saws of books, all forms, all pressures past

42 Act 3, Scene 4, lines 1429-45.

That youth and observation copied there,
And thy commandment all alone shall live
Within the book and volume of my brain,
Unmixed with baser matter. Yes, by heaven!

There seems to be another connecting word between Hamlet and one of the sonnets, a sonnet that seems to be written to Hamnet, just as the word "copy" connected *Twelfth Night* to Sonnet 11. In this case the world is "quietus," and both instances equate the silence of that word with death. In Hamlet is appears in the "To be or not to be speech," when Hamlet wonders if all his suffering "might his *quietus*[43] make/With a bare bodkin [dagger]?" That word "quietus" once again appears in Sonnet 126, addressed to "my lovely boy":

O thou, my lovely boy, who in thy pow'r
Dost hold time's fickle glass, his sickle hour,
Who hast by waning grown, and therein show'st
Thy lovers withering, as thy sweet self grow'st—
If nature, sovereign mistress over wrack,
As thou goest onwards still will pluck thee back,
She keeps thee to this purpose: that her skill
May time disgrace, and wretched minute kill.
Yet fear her, O thou minion of her pleasure;
She may detain, but not still keep, her treasure.
Her audit, though delayed, answered must be,
And her *quietus*[44] is to render thee.

---

43 Emphasis mine.

44 Emphasis mine.

Although the muse of this sonnet is traditionally, once again, often seen as the Earl of Southampton, I am not so certain. Its fixation on death and time, and the "quietus" of death seem to link it to *Hamlet*, and thus also to William's son Hamnet. As the poem seems to address a living "sweet boy," perhaps it is written about a Hamnet in declining health, giving Shakespeare's warning to "fear her," to fear death, all the more weight and dread.

Some may feel that this is all a stretch, yet I do think there is much more connective tissue between the sonnets and the plays than has yet been fully discovered. Also, Sonnet 108, again addressed to William's "sweet boy," says that "thou mine, and I thine/ Ev'n as when I first hallowed thy fair name" could yield the interpretation that when Shakespeare "first hallowed thy fair name," that could be a reference to Shakespeare first naming his son, thus *hallowing* Hamnet's name at his christening.

Yet even amidst his most intense moments of loss, tragedy, and grief, something else was growing in Shakespeare as well. Whether due to a faith crisis or a spiritual awakening, or a likely mixture of the two, Shakespeare dwells a great deal on religious questions throughout *Hamlet*.

The spiritual meditations that exist in the play begin early with Hamlet's declaration, after seeing his father's ghost, that "there are more things in heaven and earth, Horatio, than are dreamt of in your philosophy"[45]; continue through Hamlet's decision not to kill himself because of the prospect of a life after this one ("for in that sleep of death what dreams may come when we have shuffled off this mortal

45 Act 1, Scene 5, lines 168-9.

coil"[46]); and then end with the benedictory, "Good night, sweet prince, may flights of angels sing thee to thy rest."[47]

Again, there is an echo chamber between *King John* and *Hamlet*, as both hopes and fears about the afterlife seem to haunt Shakespeare's soul. Constance once again parrots what may have very well been Shakespeare's own feelings about his own departed son:

> Yes, that I will; and wherefore will I do it?
> I tore them from their bonds and cried aloud
> 'O that these hands could so redeem my son,
> As they have given these hairs their liberty!'
> But now I envy at their liberty,
> And will again commit them to their bonds,
> Because my poor child is a prisoner.
> And, father cardinal, I have heard you say
> That we shall see and know our friends in heaven:
> If that be true, I shall see my boy again;
> For since the birth of Cain, the first male child,
> To him that did but yesterday suspire,
> There was not such a gracious creature born.
> But now will canker-sorrow eat my bud
> And chase the native beauty from his cheek
> And he will look as hollow as a ghost,
> As dim and meagre as an ague's fit,
> And so he'll die; and, rising so again,
> When I shall meet him in the court of heaven

---

46 Act 3, Scene 1, lines 67-8.

47 Act 5, Scene 2, lines 358-9.

I shall not know him: therefore never, never
Must I behold my pretty Arthur more.[48]

The fact that Shakespeare uses the word "ghost" to describe Constance's dead son here, and that she has concerns that even if her son has moved to heaven, he should not be as he was here, is a distressing thought to Constance/Shakespeare. Thus, "never, never/ Must I behold my pretty Arthur more" is reflective of the strain that Elizabethans felt about their loved ones in the afterlife. After all, that paranoia and distress had been accentuated and encouraged after multitudes of years of debate, even war, over ideas like indulgences and Purgatory.

The presence of the Catholic idea of Purgatory (from where the ghost of Hamlet's father had traveled) in a play written under the reign of a Protestant monarch, has fueled a great deal of speculation, creating conspiracy theories that even question whether Shakespeare was secretly a Catholic.[49]

Whatever Shakespeare's outward religion—Catholic, Protestant, or Puritan—his inner spirituality certainly seemed to be exploring its place in the universe. Whatever his thoughts on questions of faith were before losing Hamnet, the catalyst of his son's death fueled those questions into a crucible. They would burn into his later plays, such as *King Lear* and *Macbeth*, as both

48 *King John*, Act 3, Scene 4, 1455-75.

49 Whole book length treatises on the topics of Shakespeare's secret Catholicism have been written. For example, see Claire Asquith's *Shadowplay: The Hidden Beliefs and Coded Politics of William Shakespeare* (New York: Public Affairs, 2005). Also, for an in-depth exploration of Purgatory in Halmlet and Medieval/Elizabethan society, see Stephen Greenblatt's *Hamlet in Purgatory* (Princeton and Oxford: Princeton University Press, 2002).

the light and the dark sides of the supernatural and the moral peeled his heart with the flames of an inferno.

Even these moments of faith crisis would have their tutorial benefit, however, as both his faith and his doubt would act as a refining fire, burning out the dross and purifying the silver.

LET YOUR INDULGENCE SET ME FREE

There would be an unforeseen result after Hamnet's death. Although William may have inadvertantly grown distant with Judith after Hamnet's passing, the opposite seems to have happened with Susanna: Susanna and William drew closer. Without a male heir, and with Susannah as the oldest child, the weight of their family's future now rested with her.

Thus, if we interpret Susanna as receiving high favor in her father's eyes, Hamnet's death could have been a cause. We see this shifting of familial focus within *The Winter's Tale*, where the first half of the play contains Mamillius, a beloved, young son of Leontes and Hermione. Although Leontes suspects his wife of infidelity and their once warm relationship grows cold (sound familiar?), his affection and love for his son never wavers. We see the otherwise severe Leontes share lighthearted moments with Mamillius, even playing a childish game of "I've got your nose":

> Why, that's my bawcock. What? Hast snatched thy nose?
> They say it is a copy out of mine. Come, captain.
> And yet the steer, the heifer, and the calf,

> Are all called neat.—still virginalling
> Upon his palm?—How now, you wanton calf—
> Art thou my calf?[50]

To see the often cruel and jealous Leontes turn whimsical in the company of his son is affecting, even more so when, after snatching his son's imaginary nose, he states: "it is a copy out of mine." Again, we see that echo of the word "copy" from the sonnets and *Twelfth Night*, which in both instances meant a child, specifically a child to carry on a legacy. As Leontes saw his identity play out in future generations through Mamillius, so Shakespeare saw his "copy" in Hamnet. Hamnet would be Shakespeare's heir, the endowment for future ages, the recipient of his final success, and the victor over William's enemies.

And yet, it did not come to pass. As the grief-stricken and guilt-ridden Leontes discovers of the death of Mamillius, so William discovers the death of Hamnet. The first act of *The Winter's Tale* ends as a typical Shakespearean tragedy. The innocent Hermione seems to die, Desdemona-like; Mamillius is struck down mysteriously and unexpectedly; and Leontes, who had doubted even the Oracle of Apollo's ruling of Hermione's innocence ("There is no truth at all i' the oracle:/ The sessions shall proceed: this is mere falsehood."[51]), questioning even the very gods, is now seeminly cursed by Apollo and the Pantheon ("Apollo's angry; and the heavens themselves/ Do strike at my injustice"[52]). In this, as in his earlier tragedies, Shakespeare

50 *The Winter's Tale,* Act 1, Scene 2, lines 149-50.

51 *The Winter's Tale,* Act 3, Scene 2, lines 149-50.

52 Ibid, lines 158-9

saw his life through a glass darkly: tragedy and punishment, grief and stern judgment. All that he most loved—his relationship with Anne, the joy and life of his beloved son—was destined to wither in his hands, and he couldn't even blame the gods, who had made their presence and their righteousness known to him. He could only blame himself.

And yet *The Winter's Tale* is not a tragedy. Audiences are often thrown for a loop when they come back after intermission to find that the bleak first half of the play has been replaced with a comedy that has the, literally, Bohemian vagaries of stories like *As You Like It* and *A Midsummer's Night Dream,* rather than the cataclysmic endings of *Hamlet* or *Othello* the audience had been set up to expect. The tonal shift is jarring at first, but then the weaving in of themes of redemption and resurrection climaxes in a beautiful and hopeful ending of mysterious grace.

This new format, a tragic first half mixed with a redemptive second, is part of a rising trend in Jacobean England called tragi-comedy, but which modern scholars now call Shakespeare's Romances. *The Winter's Tale* was not a romance in the modern sense, such as *While You Were Sleeping* or *Sleepless in Seattle,* focusing chiefly on a light hearted story of love (that pattern is more in keeping with Shakepeare's comedies, such as *As You Like It*), although Jacobean Romances often contain those elements as well. Rather Shakespeare's Romances are tales that blend the elements of tragedy and comedy, but then add in a mixture of the supernatural, even the spiritual, and, above all, end on a note of redemption, recociliation, and forgiveness. These Romances, like *The Winter's Tale, The Tempest, Pericles, Cym-*

beline, also tend to be family focused, with the relationships between husbands and wives, fathers and children, holding their center. Except the core relationships with children in these plays are no longer fathers and sons, as they had been in *Hamlet,* and in many of Shakespeare's histories.[53] Rather, it was now the relationship between fathers and daughters.

With the loss of Mamillius in the first half, Leontes and Hermione's daughter Perdita comes to the fore. Leontes' irrational jealousy caused him to believe that Perdita was illegitimate, and ordered her killed, but the noble Antigonus defies the order and brings the baby into Bohemia, at the sacrifice of his own life when he is killed by a bear. She is found by a Shepherd and his son, then raised by them in Bohemia. It is her forbidden romance with the Bohemian king's son and her eventual discovery of her true, royal parentage that leads to a redemptive reunion with her father.

Thus, the daughter becomes a central role in Shakespeare's latter plays, and Susanna takes that role in her father's life. She is now the heir to his legacy, literally and spiritually.

This archetypal Daughter is seen in most of Shakespeare's latter plays. *Pericles* has the tender relationship between Pericles and his kidnapped daughter Marina who proves to be resourceful, strong-willed, and spiritual; the play also includes a dark contrast to their loving relationship within the incestuous Antiochus and his daughter.

Cymbeline's familial relationships are complicated by the presence of an evil stepmother and her son that makes Snow

53 Such as the *Henry IV* plays.

White's family look like *Leave it to Beaver*. Yet the heroine Imogen fits the heroic, yet virtuous Daughter archetype. Imogen has the additional complications of a Desdemona, although she takes a more proactive approach to the accusations made against her than Desdemona ever had the chance to accomplish.

And, finally, perhaps most significantly, we have Prospero and Miranda in *The Tempest*. This is possibly the most protective relationship of the bunch, due to the trauma Miranda endured as an exile, castaway, and a victim of the attempted sexual assault of Caliban. To her credit, Miranda is still able to defy her father in the name of love, showing a worthy independent streak, while still maintaining her close relationship with him.

Prospero may sometimes come across as the overprotective father, yet their relationship is also one of the most lovingly parental relationships in Shakespeare's canon. Despite being surprised at his aggressive behavior towards her would-be suitor Sebastian, which ends up being a canny ruse on Prospero's part anyway, Miranda never loses faith in the innate goodness of her father, despite the character flaws he struggles against.

But where is Judith in all of this? We see in *Twelfth Night* a vivid portrait of her as Viola, the emotionally loyal, resourceful, soulful, and good-natured twin who lost her brother. A comparison to Viola, one of Shakespeare's great heroines, is certainly a compliment worthy of the ages. And perhaps the beautiful reunion between the two twins at the end of that play, though unachievable for the Shakespeares in this life, was meant as a beacon of hope for a reunion in the next life.

But does Judith have a place in these later plays, in the Romances? Does she partake of this cup of Grace? Perhaps Judith was away working in a household, as Germain Greer suggests,[54] and that's why she doesn't show up in these later plays?[55] Perhaps the distance between Judith and William wasn't only emotional, but geographical? Thus, at this stage of their lives, perhaps William and Judith have even fewer chances to connect than Susanna and her father do?

Or is the answer simpler than that? Perhaps Judith and Susanna are combined into one, Shakespeare drawing from the experiences of both of his daughters. The terrifying sexual assault that Miranda, Marina, and Imogen all nearly suffer could be drawn from an experience that Susanna similarly endured, certainly. Or, perhaps miscreant characters like Caliban could have a closer parallel: Thomas Quiney.

Judith and Thomas Quiney's marriage doesn't seem to have been a loveless one, lasting for nearly 50 years until her death, as well as the birth of a few children through their union. Yet the fact that Quiney had impregnated Margaret Wheeler not long before their union, and left the mother and the child to die at its birth, rightly upset Shakespeare enough for him to cut Thomas out of his will. Do we find in Quiney, perhaps, the precursor to the wet monster Caliban, who was adopted into Prospero's family, but then Caliban betrayed them with a sexually predatory nature? Is Prospero's aggressiveness towards Caliban adapted from the personal experiences of Shakespeare,

---

54 See, "His Daughter Judith and the Quineys," *The Shakespeare Circle*.

55 This all could have an interesting relation to the plot and characters of *All's Well That End's Well*.

having had the man he trusted betray his precious daughter? Are the two daughters merged into one in this narrative, as well as both of their suitors represented? John Hall as the faithful Sebastian, Thomas Quiney as the at times sympathetic, but ultimately untrustworthy Caliban?

Perhaps then the Romance plays are indeed narratives for his whole family, including the deceased Hamnet. Is he represented by the "spirit" Ariel in *The Tempest*? Ariel means "lion of God," is another name for Jerusalem, and is also an angel in the Apocrypha. These spiritual connotations may have more significance than has yet to be given to them.

The fact that Prospero holds onto the indentured services of Ariel, despite his great love for him, could be a reflection of how Shakespeare holds onto the memory of his son. Could the release that Prospero finally gives to the nymph Ariel, his airy spirit, be Shakespeare's final farewell to his "sweet boy,"[56] the one he refers to as "thee my true spirit"[57] in Sonnet 108, and refers as his "brave spirit"[58] in *The Tempest*. Could the obvious love that exists between Ariel and Prospero not be erotic, as some scholars have suggested, but rather be the love that a father has for the memory of his lost son? In Prospero giving up his magic to sail back home for good, does Shakespeare also finally find closure with the pain of failing his beloved boy Hamnet?

The importance of the redemptive themes of Shakespeare's Romances, especially as they are written at the end of his life, cannot be overstated. Throughout these last plays of Shake-

56 Sonnet 108, line 5

57 Line 2.

58 Act 1, Scene 2, line 208.

speare's he moves on from the cathartic grief and punishment he inflicted upon himself, and allows that catharsis to transform his life into something redemptive and beautiful.

In *The Winter's Tale* and *Cymbeline* we see women, falsely accused of infidelity and inconstancy, redeemed and justified, representing at long last the redemption of Anne and William's once loving relationship. We see a literal resurrection of that love, thought dead, in both the magically transforming statue of Hermione at the end of *The Winter's Tale*, and with Pericles' beloved Thaisa's dead body being drawn from the water, only to discover that it is still, indeed, alive. Love lost is now love won, and the symbolic resurrection of Anne and William's love is vividly reborn.

In *The Tempest*, a trapped spirit is akin to a dead son's memory that seemed to keep the boy's spirit trapped on earth. In freeing the nymph's spirit to the elements, he also freed his own son's soul to fly to Elysium.

In *A Winter's Tale, Pericles, The Tempest*, and *Cymbeline,* we see Regan and Goneril redeemed into the forms of Perdita, Marina, Miranda, and Imogen, daughters who are no longer overlooked and mistrusted, but rather step forward as capable, intelligent, industrious, and spiritual women ready to love their men, love their children, love life, and love themselves. Susanna and Judith both stepped forward thus, and their names are still passed down through history.

Redemption is granted even to the monsters, to finally reveal the humanity beneath their wet flesh. Prospero's enemies, even though some of them harmed those who were closest to him, receive his sincere forgiveness. Prospero's brother that took away his dukedom, the king who conspired against him, the king's brother who would conspire to betray them all, they are frankly forgiven.

Even Caliban, the creature Prospero loved like a son and the person who Miranda loved like a friend—whom they both had trusted, but then he betrayed them—even this Caliban has a glimmer of hope at the end of the play. When freed by Prospero with his "pardon,"[59] no longer a slave but once again a citizen of the island, Caliban pledges: "I'll be wise hereafter/ And seek for grace."[60] Caliban looks to his man in the moon and may finally find it smiling on him as he moves forward with the determination to be better. Though Prospero did not deny the wheels of justice that punished the creature who assaulted his daughter, yet he held out hope for Caliban yet. Thus, Shakespeare may have felt the same hope for Thomas Quiney, all while trying to protect Judith and the rest of his family from his impetuous crimes.

In this story of *The Tempest*, what most consider to be his final, non-collaborative play, Shakespeare—as his last act—asks his audience to forgive one last person: himself. In the epilogue, the wizard Prospero—a nearly transparent stand-in for Shakespeare himself—stands before the audience alone. Prospero has given up his magic, his art, to travel back home for good, leaving behind the magical island that had held so much for him, and which he ruled both with perfect love and imperfect rage. Prospero has committed to "break" his magical staff, and "drown" his book of spells, and will go home to

59 *The Tempest*, Act 5, Scene 1, lines 308.

60 *Ibid*, lines 309-10.

Milan—to Stratford upon Avon—to remain with his family for the rest of his days.

Yet before he does, he asks us to give the pardon that he has now granted to "the deceiver" in his own life. Having given mercy, he asks for it in return. Without this grace, there is no wind in his sails to get him home, and his "project fails." Having now given up the spirits that enact his will, if Prospero can't achieve this grace, his "ending is despair." His only hope is to be "relieved by prayer" which:

> ... pierces so that it assaults
> Mercy itself and frees all faults.
> As you from crimes would pardoned be,
> Let your indulgence set me free.[61]

It is a worthy, affecting ending to Shakespeare's powerful stint as an author. It is also a worthy, affecting epitaph for his life with his family, as he sought for grace, and sought to find the place within himself where he could give it in return. In these last plays, Prospero, Cymbeline, Pericles, and Leontes are all imperfect men, with their dirty humanity still clinging to them. Yet the crucible of their experiences softened them, transformed them, and Shakespeare presents himself with them and then asks for our prayers on their behalf.

CONCLUSION

As I wrote *The Drownéd Book,* I couldn't shake the feeling that I was being haunted by Shakespeare's ghost. It wasn't an eerie feeling. If anything, it was comforting. However, I laughed it off as vain, not to mention a little crazy. Yet the feeling persisted.

61 *The Tempest*, Act 5, Epilogue, lines 7-20.

Like the ghost of King Hamlet to his son, this spirit was instructive. The form and iambic pentameter came easier to me than it had before, the language flowed more smoothly, I felt more confident in the project. I felt as if Shakespeare was assisting me, encouraging me, giving me insight that I wouldn't have had otherwise. Of course, the work was still mine, and I am responsible for the interpretations and conclusions I make. Yet I felt that Shakespeare's spirit was pleased with me and with the work.

Like Hamlet, I may or may not be stark raving mad. Yet this particular project has been serendipitous from the outset. When I began, I didn't realize that I was embarking on the project during the lead up to the 400th anniversary of Shakespeare's death. That realization came later. By the time a draft was finished, we had the great fortune to be able to time its first staged reading for April 23, 2016, the 400th anniversary of Shakespeare's death. I'm still giddy that it worked out like that.

During the rehearsals and the outdoor productions for the play's first run, even Nature seemed to lend her aid, as the Moon would peek out just in time for Judith and Thomas Quiney to discuss its glowing form, or the wind would pick up right on cue for two characters' major argument. It was enchanting, and it all certainly seemed supernatural in the moment. "There is more in heaven and earth..." I have often found myself whispering under my breath.

That I was even able to cast my own 11-year-old son as the ghost of Shakespeare's 11-year-old son was particularly poignant for me. And it's perhaps not a coincidence that my beloved wife's name is also Anne. The reflections, parallels, and personal connections kept folding in on themselves, and they have buoyed me up since then, even through moments of trauma and personal tragedy.

Perhaps, like Macbeth, I am just being superstitious. Yet, also like Macbeth, I had a hard time discerning what was happening because it was fated to happen, and what was being pushed forward by own stubborn will and creative effort. In any case, the entire process has been one of the most enchantingly beautiful in my life. Like a dream haunted by fairies and nymphs.

And yet I'm not done. I'm still hungry to learn more, write more, research more, experience more, understand more of Shakespeare's life and works. This will eventually all become my Stratford Cycle, a series of plays written in the same style, and that will explore Shakespeare's life and work further.

I suppose that my personal search for Shakespeare may stretch over my whole life. I am certainly still unpacking all that I learned through this process. I've researched, I've pondered, I've theorized, and I've realized how much I still don't know.

Bradley Moss as William Shakespeare and Hyrum Stewart as Hamnet's Ghost (background). Photo by Emily Drew.

Printed in Great Britain
by Amazon

79547770R00102